A SURVEY OF THE BIBLE

Training for Service

LEADER'S GUIDE

by ORRIN ROOT

Revised By Eleanor Daniel

STANDARD
PUBLISHING
Cincinnati, Ohio

How to Conduct the Course

Training for Service—A Survey of the Bible has proved to be immensely popular among church leaders since its first publication in 1907. It appeals to thousands of earnest Christians who are enthusiastic about the help it gives them in their Bible study.

Many of those Christians who take the course go on to become teachers. A vast multitude of successful teachers today point to this book as the source of their first training for their work. In fact, that was its original primary design.

In planning a course of study in this text, therefore, the first step is to decide to whom it will be offered. Sometimes a class is composed entirely of teachers, of prospective teachers, of new Christians, of church officers, of young people, or of a single Sunday school class. More often, however, a church simply offers the course to all who wish to take it.

If no *Training for Service* class is available, an individual may complete this course as an independent or correspondence study. That person must choose a teacher, minister, or other qualified person to administer the final exam and grade it. The chosen person will sign and present a certificate to the student who has received a grade of 70% or more on the final exam or exams. The free certificate must be requested from Standard Publishing, c/o Christian Ministries Department, 8121 Hamilton Ave., Cincinnati, OH 45231.

Enrolling the Students

If the course is to be offered to a special group, a meeting of that group may provide the best opportunity to promote the course and enroll students. Or a few enthusiastic people may ask each member personally.

If the class is to be open to all, it should be well publicized. Announcements may be made from the pulpit, in Sunday school classes, in the church paper or bulletin, by means of posters, letters, telephone calls, and personal visits. It may be wise for the minister and Sunday school superintendent to make a special effort to enroll people who may become teachers in the future.

Selecting the Instructor

The best instructor available should be asked to lead the class. Desirable qualifications are Christian character, Bible knowledge, and teaching ability, yet these lessons are so arranged that they may be used without an experienced instructor. Someone who has taken the course before may be asked to be the leader; or, if necessary, the class may choose one of its own members to lead its study.

Securing Materials

Each member of the class should have a Bible and his own copy of *Training for Service—A Survey of the Bible*. The instructor should have the Instructor's edition of this book.

Revised ©1996 by Standard Publishing, Cincinnati, Ohio. A division of Standex International Corporation. All rights reserved. Printed in U.S.A.

Library of Congress Cataloging in Publication Data

Root, Orrin.
   Training for service.
   At head of title: Instructor.
   Summary: A survey of the contents of the Bible including historical sidelights and suggestions for teaching.
   1. Bible—Textbooks. 2. Bible—Criticism, interpretation, etc. [I. Bible—Study] I. Daniel, Eleanor Ann. II. Title.

[BS605.2.R67 1983b]   220.6'1   83-4677
ISBN 0-87239-703-3

04   03

An overhead projector would be a helpful piece of equipment for this course, especially for large classes. A chalkboard and a bulletin board will also be helpful to the instructor's success.

Student activity worksheets are included on pages [33] through [43] of this Instructor book. These may be photocopied for each student.

The exams, found at the conclusion of this Instructor book, may be copied for each student. You may choose to use either the final exam or the two exams (lessons 1 through 13 and lessons 14 through 26). If you choose to use the two exams, give the first exam after completion of lesson 13 and the second one after completion of lesson 26. After grading the exam/exams, the instructor will present a certificate to each student with a grade of 70% or above. The free certificates must be requested by writing to Standard Publishing, c/o Christian Ministries Department, 8121 Hamilton Ave., Cincinnati, Ohio 45231.

To the Instructor

So you are the instructor for a class in *Training for Service—A Survey of the Bible.* Congratulations! You have been given a vote of confidence and an important trust.

Perhaps you are a trained and experienced instructor. In that case your task will not be difficult. You easily could teach such a simple course without the suggestions offered in this instructor's section. Nevertheless you may find it worthwhile to read the following pages. You will find some ideas you like, and they may reduce the time you spend in planning.

Do not fall into the trap of overconfidence just because you are used to teaching. This is an unusual course. Its very simplicity gives rise to complications. Adults have grown unaccustomed to elementary learning, and some do not take to it easily. For example, we shall be learning to repeat the names of the Bible books in order. Your students could have learned this easier when they were Juniors. Now some of them will find the effort frustrating. They will say, "I'm too old to learn." It will be your task and your joy to show them that they can learn. On the other hand, some of your students probably did learn the Bible books when they were Juniors, and still remember them. They may be bored with a study of such well-known material. It will be your task to keep them interested and use their knowledge to help the others learn. You will find a need for all your skill.

Perhaps you have taken a course in *Training for Service* yourself, or perhaps you have even taught it before. That is good. It will make your task easier. You will naturally tend to teach as you have taught before. But still you may find some help in this instructor's section, particularly if you are not entirely satisfied with the familiar ways of conducting the course. Do not let your previous experience lull you into a false sense of security. Take time to study each lesson carefully and plan how to present it. Otherwise you may be surprised and humiliated by some point that has slipped your mind.

Perhaps you have no training or experience as an instructor, and perhaps you never even saw this book until you were asked to teach it. In that case you are probably scared. But don't worry. You have encouragement from several directions.

First, you can have the best help in the world. "If any of you lack wisdom, let him ask of God, that giveth to all men liberally, and upbraideth not; and it shall be given him" (James 1:5). This means you!

Second, it is encouraging to know that

[3]

thousands of people like you have already taught this course successfully. What has been done can be done.

Third, your leaders have picked you for this job because you are the best person available. Their confidence gives you confidence.

Fourth, this instructor's section is written especially for you. It suggests ideas for presenting every lesson. You will see instantly that some of these ideas will work in your class. Use them. You will suspect that some ideas are not suited to your group. Skip them. You will see some ideas that you can improve. Improve them.

Fifth, you have more ability than you know. Put it to work and watch it grow. Don't be afraid of your own ideas. Use illustrations from your own experience. Devise original teaching aids. Assign good students to prepare helpful reports. You may find that your own plans are the best ones.

One great secret of success with this course is you, the instructor. Your students depend on your full knowledge to guide them. They count on your goodwill and good judgment and good humor to make each lesson happy and effective. They expect you to be a good instructor, and you are determined not to disappoint them.

You can be a confident and competent instructor by trusting God and working diligently. Master every lesson, and then master a plan for teaching it. And talk it over with the Lord.

Preparing to Teach

If you have never taught this course before, the suggestions on these pages may be very helpful. If you are a veteran, probably you have already learned to follow a similar procedure.

It is good, of course, to study the whole book thoroughly before beginning to teach it. But if that is impossible, there is no need to worry. Just be sure to keep well ahead of the class.

1. Master each lesson. Every student ought to do this, but it is doubly necessary for you because you are the instructor. Be sure you know the facts; memorize everything that is to be memorized. Work the puzzles and quizzes. This will give you confidence and enable you to help the students. With the lesson securely in mind, you can be at ease, free to give attention to questions and to the progress of the class discussion. To increase your assurance, keep the book and your notes open during the class sessions. If some point has slipped your mind, refer to the book or notes without embarrassment.

2. Plan each class session. Read the suggested lesson plan. Research any points that need it. Review the student activity worksheets, make copies for the students, and decide how you will use them. As students arrive, they may complete this activity. The instructor may lead a discussion of the worksheet answers.

How will you introduce the lesson? How will it proceed? How will it close? What questions will you ask? What part will students take?

Since students study the lesson before the class meeting, they will be familiar with its teaching. The purpose of the class session is to reinforce their learning. You will need interesting ways to cover the material given in the textbook. You may introduce additional information. You know your class better than anyone else. Plan the session to fit it. Use the suggestions that are given, or amend them, or substitute other methods as you think best; but do be sure to get attention, hold interest, and fix the facts of the lesson in mind.

3. Look ahead. To lay plans for the next session is not enough. At that session you may want to ask some of the students to take some special part in the session that will follow. Therefore you must have your plans at least partly made for that following session. For some lessons of the course, it is suggested that you have several leaders take charge of parts of the sessions. If you use this plan, you will need to consider these lessons even longer in advance so that you can select the leaders and give them time to make their preparation. See "Student Leadership" on this page below.

4. Don't try to follow the suggestions in one-two-three order. That is, don't wait until you master the lesson before you begin to plan the class session, but do both together. As you study the lesson you will think now and then of a good visual aid, a good way to introduce the lesson discussion, or an idea for student participation. Make a note of this whenever it comes into your mind. Study the suggestions in this instructor's section, but don't be afraid to use your own ideas instead. Perhaps your lesson plan will be complete even before you have mastered the lesson yourself—but you need to master the lesson plan and the lesson.

How can you find time for thorough preparation? Only you can answer. Undoubtedly you will have to give up some of the things you would like to do. Capable teaching requires a deep interest, a devotion to the task, a willingness to sacrifice.

There is no quick and easy way to be a good instructor. But your time and effort will be rewarded as you see students growing in their understanding of the holy Scriptures.

Using Student Leadership

From almost the beginning of the course, you are encouraged to use students to assist in lesson development. Thus you can give the more promising ones a taste of teaching. Their participation can add variety to the class session and release you from the necessity of planning every detail yourself. Besides, it may reveal that some students are qualified to become teachers in the near future.

Do not think this plan will make your own work lighter. It will make it heavier. You will have to study a lesson about three weeks in advance to see how many leaders will be needed. You will have to choose the leaders a week in advance and explain to each one what is expected of him/her. You may have to guide some of them in preparing to do their parts. In short, you cannot merely appoint inexperienced leaders and then expect them to take care of everything. You will have to help them become experienced.

1. Three weeks in advance, study the lesson and the suggested lesson plan.

2. A week in advance, appoint the necessary leaders. See that each one lays his/her plans, with or without your help. Know the plans of all the leaders well enough to be sure there is not too much duplication. Be sure each leader knows just how much time is allotted to him/her.

3. When the time arrives, you may have to act as timekeeper or appoint someone else to see that no one takes too much time. When many students have prepared themselves to take part, each one must have his/her opportunity. A kitchen timer provides an impartial, non-threatening signal.

Resources

Study Helps for Instructor and Student

Halley, Henry H., *Halley's Bible Handbook,* Zondervan Publishing House.

Standard Bible Atlas, 2nd Edition, Standard Publishing, 03166*.

Tabernacle Resources

Tabernacle Model to Make, Standard Publishing, 02129*.

Tabernacle Pict-O-Graph, Standard Publishing, 02218*.

Maps and Charts

Old Testament Maps and Charts, 02607*
  The Old Testament World
  The Exodus
  The Conquest of Canaan
  The Twelve Tribes of Israel
  The Divided Kingdom
  The Assyrian Empire
  The Babylonian Empire
  The Persian Empire
  The Tabernacle
  The Modern Middle East
  The Kings and Prophets of Israel
    and Judah
  The Bible Library

New Testament Maps and Charts, 02608*
  The New Testament World
  Palestine in Jesus' Day
  Jerusalem in Jesus' Time
  Early Journeys of Apostles and
    Evangelists
  Paul's First and Second Missionary
    Journeys
  Paul's Third Journey and Voyage to
    Rome
  Modern Palestine and the New
    Testament
  The Spread of Christianity in the First
    Century
  Herod's Temple
  The Land of the Jews in the Time
    Between the Testaments
  The Books of the New Testament
  The "Many Convincing Proofs" of the
    Resurrection

Time Lines

(Post one of these on the bulletin board throughout the course of study)

Bible Time Line, Standard Publishing, 02628*.

Simplified Bible Time Line, Standard Publishing, 02604*.

*Number indicates the Standard Publishing catalog order number of the product.

Lesson 1—How We Got Our Bible

Attention

Arrange to have a display of various Bible versions for the students to examine as they arrive. Include at least a Greek New Testament, King James Version, American Standard Version, Revised Standard Version, New English Bible, Today's English Version, New American Standard Version, New International Version, and New King James Version. Other old versions will be interesting, if they are available. Be sure to label each Bible using its correct title. Place a card or direction sheet on the table that includes these instructions: "Look up a familiar verse or passage such as John 3:16 in each version (except the Greek New Testament, unless you know Greek). Read the passage and compare the wording from version to version. Do different wordings alter the basic message?" Allot five to seven minutes past the beginning time for this activity to be completed.

Introduce the Bible survey course upon which the class is embarking. Explain the following questions for today's lesson: How did we get our Bible? How did it begin? How has it been handed down to us? It will be the basis for today's lesson.

Discovery

Form groups of three. Assign each group the following Scriptures: 1 Corinthians 2:13; 1 Thessalonians 2:13; 2 Timothy 3:16; 2 Peter 1:20, 21; and Revelation 22:18, 19. Instruct each group to read the verses and find the answer to this question: What does the Bible say about its authorship and purpose? Allow five minutes for this; then discuss their findings. Emphasize that *all*

Scripture—every bit—is God-breathed.

Discuss, either in small groups or the larger group, this assignment: define inspiration. After the discussion, share this definition: Inspiration is God's revelation communicated to us through writers who used their own minds and words, yet God so directed their lives and thoughts that the words they used in writing were the very words of God. Emphasize that forty writers wrote the Bible over a period of 1,500 years.

Give a brief lecture of the material "Ancient Versions and Manuscripts."

Let the students share their findings from the "Attention" step.

Allow time for questions.

Summarize today's session.

Conclusion

Lead a time of prayer in which you give thanks to God for inspired revelation that has been preserved through the centuries so we can enjoy the Bible even today.

Assignment

Remind the students that the key to the success of this class is for each person to come to class prepared. Encourage them to answer the questions at the end of each chapter during the week.

Ask one student to prepare a short presentation about the nature of and need for authority. He/she should use the "God Speaks With Authority" section from Lesson 2 and expand upon it by using Matthew 7:24-29; John 12:48, 49; Nehemiah 8:2, 3, 8 and other resources.

Ask another student to prepare a short presentation from the section "The Bible as God's Word" from Lesson 2.

[7]

Lesson 2—God's Word to Us

Attention

Write the following statement on the chalkboard: ". . . ultimately the question of the authority of Scriptures is a matter of faith and not of argument" (Martin Lloyd-Jones). Group the class members by threes and ask them to decide whether they agree or disagree with the statement and why. Give each group a piece of paper and a felt-tip marker to record their answer and reasons. Allow five or six minutes for this work and reports.

Discovery

Begin this section of the lesson by inviting the individual assigned to present his/her report on the nature and need for authority. Be prepared to mention any material from the text that was omitted. Follow this with the assigned report, "The Bible as God's Word." Again, add any omitted text material.

Then ask the students to turn to Philemon in their Bibles. Explain that the class will do a study using the principles mentioned. Distribute the worksheets you photocopied from the worksheet original. (To be ready to help students, you should have worked through the process yourself.) Allow fifteen minutes for class members to work in groups of five to read the book and answer questions 1, 2, and two others as assigned. Let the groups report their results.

Emphasize the importance of the trustworthy nature of the Bible so that Bible principles can apply to today. Then discuss the following questions:

1. Why must we regard the Bible as authoritative if we are to gain the most from its study?
2. How does reading the total context help you in your study?

Worksheet for Philemon

1. Read the entire book of Philemon.
2. Who wrote the book of Philemon?
3. To whom was Philemon written?
4. Write the key words in the text.
5. Develop a brief outline of the book.
6. Write a one-sentence summary for each section of the outline.
7. Summarize the problem addressed in the book.
8. What was the intended meaning of verses 17-21?
9. What principles for living today does this book present?

---

3. How do the principles of study discussed today help you?

Conclusion

Summarize the day's session. Encourage the students to begin to incorporate these Bible study principles into their Bible study this week. Close with prayer.

Assignment

Encourage each student to read Lesson 3 before the next class session.

Ask for volunteers to read one book from each section of the Bible. Each volunteer should read a different book. One could read Genesis, a second Ruth, a third Ecclesiastes, and a fourth Micah. Another group of students can read from the New Testament: one Mark, one Acts, one 1 John, and one Revelation. Ask each to come with a brief summary of the content of the book he/she read.

Encourage all class members to begin reading the Old Testament this week.

Lesson 3—Divisions of the Bible

Attention

As the class members arrive, give them copies of the matching exercise. Allot five minutes for this activity. Students can check their work from their Bibles or textbooks if they finish before you are ready to proceed. Go over the correct answers. Then remind the class that today's lesson deals with an overview of the composition of the Bible.

Match Them

Old	1. Collection of 39 books.
Old	2. Five books of law.
New	3. Four gospels.
New	4. One book of prophecy.
Old	5. Five books of poetry.
New	6. Twenty-one letters.
New	7. Collection of 27 books.
Old	8. Seventeen books of prophecy.
New	9. One book of history.
Old	10. Twelve books of history.

Discovery

Draw an open Bible on the chalkboard. Point out that this book, the Bible, is composed of sixty-six books grouped into two major divisions, the Old Testament and the New Testament. Each division is further subdivided into four parts.

Outline the four divisions of the Old Testament on the left side of the Bible. Include the number of books in each. Ask the person who read a book from each section to give a one- or two-sentence summary of the types of literature included in that section. Add interesting facts from the textbook material. When you have completed the overview, have class members recite together the names of the divisions and numbers of books.

Repeat the same procedure for the New Testament division.

Now play a game to make sure the students have the information firmly in mind. Draw eight squares on the chalkboard as shown below. Explain that these represent the four groups of books in the Old Testament and in the New Testament. Ask them to name the groups in unison as you point to each square.

Divide the class into two teams. You will name a player whose turn it is to play. Point to one of the squares and ask either, "What kind?" or "How many?" When you ask, "What kind?" the player is to name the division of the Bible. When you ask, "How many?" the player gives the number of books in the group. A correct answer must be given within ten seconds and will count a point for the team. Make sure each player gets at least one turn.

Then continue by having the student give a fact about the division selected. Any correct information is acceptable except for "what kind" and "how many." A fact once used cannot be repeated. Follow the same time and scoring guidelines as before.

Continue playing until you have no more time or no more information can be supplied about any division.

Conclusion

Summarize the lesson for today. Review the divisions of the Bible again. Then read Romans 12 as an example of the letters written to guide our Christian living. Lead a closing prayer.

Assignment

Ask class members to read Lesson 4 for next week. Encourage them to begin to memorize the names of the books of the Old Testament. Ask them to read one book of the Old Testament during the week. You may want to ask each person to read a different book so each can assist in next week's presentation.

Lesson 4—Books of the Old Testament

Attention

Photocopy the word-find puzzle to give one to each person as he/she enters the classroom. Ask each to see how many names of the Old Testament books he/she can find. This will reinforce familiarity with the names of the books of the Old Testament. Allot ten minutes for this activity. Display a completed puzzle on an overhead transparency or on a poster for the students to check their answers.

The Old Testament Books

```
A D E C C L E S I A S T E S U W P
H A X T H U H A I M E H E N R L R
A N O V O H A G B N A H U M I K O
I I D B S J J E J U D G E S S A V
D E U T E R O N O M Y E Z R A S E
A L S O A M N E B U H A C I M S R
B J O S H U A S A C H R O N U E B
O H A B B A H I M R E H T S E L S
E L P S A L M S O Z O J O E L C K
L E V I T I C U S O X W Y R L I U
K I O S N O G U S R E B M U N N K
I K N A Z E C H A R I A H T W O K
N E L I H A I N A H P E Z H O R A
G Z L A M E N T A T I O N S O H B
S E O H A G G A I Y Z N O T S C A
H A I M E R E J M A L A C H I A H
E G C N O M O L O S F O G N O S B
```

Make the transition into the next section by pointing out that today's lesson deals with the books of the Old Testament and the basic content of each.

Discovery

Quickly review the names of the four sections of the Old Testament.

Begin with the books of law. Call on various class members to supply the names of the books in order. As they do, you or a student write the abbreviations of the names on a chalkboard, poster board, or transparency. Ask class members to summarize the contents of each book as you go. (Those who read a particular book during the week could do this.) Add any information not covered by the students. Do the same with the books of history, poetry, and prophecy. Be careful to pace yourself as you go so that all of the Old Testament can be covered during the session.

Go over the list of book names several times section by section repeating the books in unison. Then go around the class, with each student naming a book. Time this and see if the time can be shortened when the process is repeated.

Closing

You may want to prepare a handout sheet to distribute to your class to list the books of the Old Testament and to summarize the contents. (*Halley's Bible Handbook* would be a good resource.) If so, do it now instead of earlier in order to maintain individual attention to class activity.

Briefly summarize the lesson for today. Then close with prayer.

Assignment

Encourage students to complete the task of memorizing the names of the books of the Old Testament.

Ask the class members to read Lesson 5 for next week. Encourage them to begin work to master the names of the New Testament books.

Ask the class members to read one book of the New Testament during the coming week. As you did last week, you may want to ask each person to read a different book so each can have something to contribute during next week's presentation. Send an assignment sheet around, permitting each person to choose his/her reading. Instruct each person to be prepared with a one- or two-sentence summary of the book's contents.

Lesson 5—Books of the New Testament

Attention

As the class members arrive, give them copies of the crossword puzzle. Ask them to complete as much as they can before you are ready to proceed with the lesson. Display a completed puzzle on a chart or a transparency for the class members to check themselves.

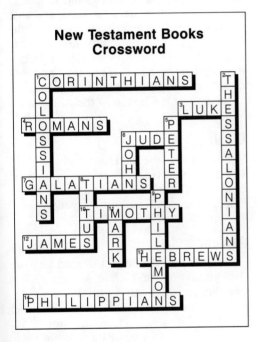

New Testament Books Crossword

Discovery

Review the four sections of the New Testament. Use last week's chart to keep the sections before the students.

Begin with the Gospels. Call on class members to supply the names. As they do, write the name or its abbreviation as you did with the Old Testament books. Ask those who read a book to summarize the content of each book as you go. Add any pertinent information. Do the same with the book of history, a letter, and the book of prophecy.

Go over the names of the New Testament books in unison a time or two. Also review the sections and names of the Old Testament books.

Closing

If you distributed an Old Testament summary sheet last week, you will want to do the same for the New Testament books. Briefly summarize the lesson for the day. Close with prayer.

Assignment

Ask the class members to read Lesson 6 before class time next week. Encourage them to continue reading through the Bible and to work on memorization of the names of the books of the Bible.

Select three leaders to prepare presentations for the three dispensations of Bible history. They should use textbook material, but may also use *Halley's Bible Handbook*. They will have ten minutes each for their presentations.

Lesson 6—Three Dispensations

Attention

As the class members arrive, give each person a copy of the statements below or write them on the chalkboard or a transparency. Ask students to form groups of three and discuss their responses.

AGREE OR DISAGREE

Decide if you agree or disagree with each statement below. Be prepared to explain/defend your answer to two other people.

1. Since worship has occurred in different ways throughout history with God's blessing, God will probably change it again. Agree/Disagree
2. The Old Testament isn't very important to a Christian. Agree /Disagree
3. God's way of dealing with people will probably change in the future. Agree/Disagree

Allow ten minutes for response and small-group discussion. Then take a few minutes for a large-group discussion centered on the responses.

Discovery

Begin with a game to review the sections and names of the Bible books. Divide into two groups. The first person in the first group must name the first section of the Old Testament. The first person in the other group names the first book of the first section. Go back and forth from team to team, first naming all law books, then identifying the second section and its books, then naming the third section and its books, and finally identifying the fourth section and its books. Follow the same

pattern for the New Testament. (If a person answers incorrectly, go to the other team.) Each correct answer is worth one point. Spend no more than ten minutes on this game.

Read Hebrews 1:1, 2 to introduce the idea of dispensations. Let the three speakers present their reports. Time them so that no speaker exceeds ten minutes. After the speakers have finished, add any omitted details. Then display a time line like the one at the bottom of this page on a poster. Point out how all of the information fits together. Have the students duplicate this time line in the blank space at the end of the lesson in their books.

Closing

Summarize the material for the day. Use any extra time to review the names of the books of the Bible and the three dispensations. Close with prayer.

Assignment

Ask the class members to read Lesson 7 prior to the next class session. Also encourage them to continue reading through the Bible. Ask them to become familiar with each place mentioned in Lesson 7 and to find it on a Bible map because they will be expected to be able to do so in class next week. Encourage them to practice by drawing a map and locating the places mentioned in the lesson. You may want to recommend *Standard Bible Atlas* to assist the students in their study.

Explain that if they have the map well enough in mind to draw it from memory, they can instantly visualize many of the Old Testament movements.

Lesson 7—The Old Testament World

Attention

As the students arrive, give each person a copy of the matching exercise. Ask them to do as much as they can until you are ready to proceed.

Display the correct answers on a chart or go over the answers together. Then point out that these are the places of the Old Testament world that form the basis of today's lesson.

Match Them

D	1. Tigris	**B**	9. Israel
B	2. Egypt	**C**	10. Sinai
C	3. Ararat	**D**	11. Euphrates
B	4. Babylonia	**D**	12. Nile
C	5. Nebo	**B**	13. Persia
A	6. Red Sea	**C**	14. Carmel
A	7. Great Sea	**D**	15. Jordan
B	8. Assyria		

Discovery

Give each person a copy of the blank map you made from the map on page [36]. Ask each person to fill in his/her map as you present the material today, using a large Old Testament World map. You may write in names as you talk.

Point out the east end of the Mediterranean (called the Great Sea in the Old Testament) with the Nile River flowing into it from Egypt. To the southeast is the two-horned end of the Red Sea. To the northeast is the head of the Euphrates River that flows through Mesopotamia to the Persian Gulf. Near the Euphrates is the Tigris River. Be sure to identify every place mentioned in today's lesson in the text: rivers, bodies of water, mountains, empires, and special places.

Closing

Summarize today's material. Use any extra time to review material from previous lessons.

Assignment

Ask the students to read Lesson 8. Ask eight volunteers to prepare a three-minute report each on one of the eight major characters in the lesson. The report might include:
1. Identify the person, giving the main events of his life.
2. Tell his strengths and weaknesses.
3. Identify people associated with his life.
4. Tell how God used this person in His plan.

Lesson 8—Old Testament People, Part One

Attention

Before the students begin to arrive, write the following statement on the chalkboard, a transparency, or a poster: "A Christian should study the Old Testament because . . ." Ask each person to write a completion to the sentence and share it with three other people. Then lead a general discussion to develop a list of reasons for studying the Old Testament.

Make the transition into today's lesson by leading a brief review of the previous five lessons. Point out that today's lesson deals with eight of the sixteen major characters of the Old Testament.

Discovery

Proceed with the eight presentations assigned last week. Time each so that no speaker exceeds three minutes. A kitchen timer may help.

Closing

Use any extra time to play a game. The first person names the first major character, the next a lesser character, the next a place, and the next an event. Do this for all eight major characters. Each person who gives a correct answer receives one point.

Assignment

Ask the students to read Lesson 9 before the next class. Get eight more volunteers (preferably different ones from this week) to make three-minute reports on the final eight major Old Testament characters. Encourage all students to continue memorizing Bible sections and books, dispensations, and characters.

Character	Lesser Characters	Place	Event	
ADAM	Cain Abel	Mesopotamia	Creation Sin	PATRIARCHAL
NOAH	Ham Shem Japheth	Mesopotamia	Flood	
ABRAHAM	Lot Isaac Jacob	Mesopotamia Canaan	Promise	
JOSEPH	Reuben Benjamin Pharaoh	Canaan Egypt	Slavery	
MOSES	Pharaoh Aaron Jethro	Egypt Sinai	Exodus Wilderness Wandering	JEWISH
JOSHUA	Caleb Eleazer Rahab	Sinai Canaan	Promised Land	
GIDEON	Samson Deborah Ruth	Canaan	Judges	
SAMUEL	Hannah Eli Joel Abiah	Canaan	Anointing of David	

Lesson 9—Old Testament People, Part Two

Attention

As the students arrive, give each a copy of the word-find puzzle. Hidden in it are the names of sixteen major Old Testament characters.

Display a completed puzzle on a chalkboard, poster, or transparency, and have the students check themselves.

Discovery

Move on into the biographical presentations. Be sure that no presentation exceeds three minutes.

Closing

Use any extra time to play the game suggested for last week, using the new list of eight characters.

Assignment

Ask the students to study Lesson 10 for the next class session. Encourage them to read each Scripture passage listed. Also ask them to memorize the periods of Old Testament history mentioned at the beginning of the lesson. Get six volunteers to prepare four-minute reports on the six events covered in Lesson 10.

Find Them

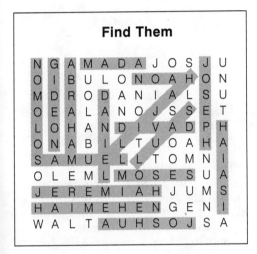

Character	Lesser Characters	Place	Event	
SAUL	Kish Jonathan Abner	Canaan	First King	
DAVID	Goliath Nathan Absalom	Jerusalem	Great King	
SOLOMON	Queen of Sheba Rehoboam Jeroboam	Jerusalem	Wisdom	
ELIJAH	Jezebel Ahab Elisha	Israel	Prophets of Baal Mt. Carmel	JEWISH
ISAIAH	Sennacherib Hezekiah Manasseh	Israel	Foretold Coming of Christ	
JEREMIAH	Huldah Jehoiakim Zedekiah	Judah	Captivity of Judah	
DANIEL	Nebuchadnezzar Belshazzar Cyrus	Babylon	Advisor to Kings	
NEHEMIAH	Artaxerxes Ezra Malachi	Jerusalem	Rebuilt City Walls	

Lesson 10—Old Testament Periods, Part One

Attention

Give each person a copy of the review acrostic. The first letters of the answers will spell today's topic.

```
┌─────────────────────────────────┐
│        Review Acrostic          │
│                                 │
│   1. O B A D I A H              │
│   2. L E T T E R S              │
│   3. D E C L I N E              │
│                                 │
│   4. T I G R I S                │
│   5. E Z R A                    │
│   6. S O L O M O N              │
│   7. T I M O T H Y              │
│   8. A S S Y R I A              │
│   9. M E S O P O T A M I A      │
│  10. E S T H E R                │
│  11. N E H E M I A H            │
│  12. T H E S S A L O N I A N S  │
│                                 │
│  13. P R O B A T I O N          │
│  14. E G Y P T                  │
│  15. R E D E M P T I O N        │
│  16. I S A I A H                │
│  17. O L D   T E S T A M E N T  │
│  18. D A N I E L                │
│  19. S E R V I T U D E          │
└─────────────────────────────────┘
```

Allow up to ten minutes for the students to complete this. Then go over the answers together.

Discovery

Draw on a poster board or transparency the chart from page 51 in the student section of this book. Encourage the six leaders to fill in the correct portion of the chart as they present their reports. Be sure that reports are limited to four minutes.

Probation
Fall	
Promise	Adam
Flood	Noah

Preparation
Dispersion	
Journeys	Abraham
Egypt	Joseph

Divide the class into six small groups. Ask each to develop a one-minute sermon to answer: What does this period of history teach us? Assign one period to each group. Allot five minutes for them to prepare, then a minute each for the presentations.

Closing

Use any extra time to review the information in Lessons 3-9. Use review questions from these lessons to assist you. Close with prayer.

Assignment

Ask the students to read Lesson 11 before the next class session. Encourage them to continue reading the Old Testament by reading at least one more book this week. Find six more volunteers to prepare four-minute reports on the six events covered in Lesson 11. Encourage class members to review the material covered during the course in order to fix facts in their memories.

Lesson 11—Old Testament Periods, Part Two

Attention

As the students enter, ask them to complete this sentence (which you have written on the chalkboard or a transparency): "Bible study is important for me because . . ." Ask each person to complete the sentence in at least three ways, then share his/her responses with a group of three other people. Allow the groups five to seven minutes for discussion before leading a general discussion centered on the assigned theme. List the reasons presented on the chalkboard or transparency.

Continue the discussion by asking: Why is this course of study important? What have you gained from it so far? List these suggestions as well. Then make the transition into today's material by pointing out that two more periods of Bible history will be studied.

Discovery

Display the poster or transparency you used last week. This week the reporters will add the details for two more periods of Old Testament history. Have the reporters go in turn to present their material. Be sure that they do not exceed the four-minute limit.

Conquest

Wilderness	Moses
Canaan	Joshua
Judges	Gideon
	Samuel

Power

Saul's Defeat	Saul
David's Capital	David
Solomon's Temple	Solomon

After the reports are completed, divide the class into six groups. Assign one of the six events to each group. Instruct each group to decide what major lesson is to be learned from the event. Instruct them to put this into a commercial jingle to sing to the rest of the class in order to encourage them to heed this lesson Scripture. Encourage them to select the tune of a commonly known jingle. Allow up to ten minutes for them to decide upon the lesson and to compose the jingle. Then have each group share its jingle with the entire group. Take a few minutes to emphasize the importance of heeding these lessons.

Closing

Prepare a "pep talk" conclusion to this session. Emphasize the value of Bible study and the importance of having a firm grasp of background details as an aid to understanding the Biblical text. Praise the students who have prepared faithfully during the first eleven weeks. Encourage them to continue their careful preparation. Urge others to follow their example. Close with prayer.

Assignment

Ask class members to read and prepare Lesson 12 prior to the next session. Encourage them to review Lessons 1-11 so they can recall and/or identify the books of the Bible as well as major geographical areas and sites, major characters, and the periods of history from the Old Testament. (The questions on page 50 in the student book will aid in doing this.)

Get six volunteers to prepare four-minute reports on the six events included in Lesson 12.

The Old Testament Maps and Charts packet (02607) contains several maps that will be helpful with these reports: The Divided Kingdom, The Assyrian Empire, The Babylonian Empire, and The Persian Empire. See the kings and prophets chart on page 49 in the student book. See pages 62 and 63 for more information on the time between the Testaments.

Encourage all class members to continue reading the Old Testament books. Urge them especially to read the Biblical accounts of each event in the lesson.

Lesson 12—Old Testament Periods, Part Three

Attention

As the students enter the classroom, give each a copy of "Match Them." Ask them to match the people with the periods.

Allot six to eight minutes for this. Go over the correct answers with the class, then make the transition into the lesson for today.

Discovery

Display the poster or transparency from the two previous lessons. The final portions will be filled in today.

Have the six students make their reports. Adhere rigidly to the time limitations.

Decline

Division	Elijah
Fall of Northern Kingdom	Isaiah
Fall of Southern Kingdom	Jeremiah

Servitude

Babylonian Rule	Daniel
Persian Rule	Nehemiah
Greek Rule	Ezra
Egyptian Rule	Malachi
Syrian Rule	
Maccabean Freedom	
Roman Rule	

Draw a blank chart on the board or on a transparency. Let the class members go in turn to the chart and fill in one detail. The first person must write the name of a period. The next adds an event or person from that period. The third does the same. Continue until the details about a period are completed. Then the name of a new period may be added and its details completed. Proceed until the chart is finished. If you desire, make this a team competition.

Closing

Lead a brief discussion centered on this topic: What lessons can we learn from each period of history? Close with prayer.

Assignment

Ask the students to read Lesson 13 before the next session. Encourage the students to continue reading the Old Testament.

Ask a volunteer to make a special study of the tabernacle and prepare a visual drawn to scale and showing the location of each part. A resource is available for the volunteer to make a model of the tabernacle: 02129, *Tabernacle Model to Make*. You may wish to use the *Tabernacle Pict-O-Graph*, 02218.

Another volunteer may prepare a report on the altar and the sacrificial system. Encourage the person to read Leviticus to find a description of the various sacrifices.

Match Them

D	1. Abraham	D	10. Joseph
E	2. Adam	A	11. Joshua
F	3. Daniel	F	12. Malachi
C	4. David	A	13. Moses
B	5. Elijah	F	14. Nehemiah
F	6. Ezra	E	15. Noah
A	7. Gideon	A	16. Samuel
B	8. Isaiah	C	17. Saul
B	9. Jeremiah	C	18. Solomon

Lesson 13—Altar and Tabernacle

Attention

As the students arrive, have them form groups of three. Then ask the groups to prepare an acrostic for "Worship." Give them the following directions:

"Today we begin a study of Old Testament worship. Notice the letters I have written on the chalkboard spelling *worship*. How many words or phrases can you think of beginning with these seven letters that describe something about worship? For example O could stand for orderly. In your group see how many words you can get." A sample acrostic is included below.

W orthy God
O rderly
R eal
S inging
H eavenward
I n Jesus' name
P raise

After five minutes, invite class members to share their responses as you write them on the chalkboard or a transparency. Then make the transition into the lesson theme for the day.

Discovery

Let the reporter who studied the sacrificial system and the altar present his findings. Be prepared to fill in the details if necessary. Be sure that the students understand the purpose of the sacrificial system.

Distribute to the students a scale drawing of the tabernacle like the one on page 53 in the student book. Tell the students that they can fill in the drawing as the lesson is developed. Have the volunteer who studied the tabernacle dimensions and systems present his report at this time. Add any details not covered by the report. Be sure that the students understand the symbolism for each part of the tabernacle.

Have the class members identify a part or piece of furniture in the tabernacle. Ask students to tell about size, materials, use, and symbolism.

Lead a discussion answering these questions: Why did God give so much attention to the worship system in the Old Testament? What lessons can we learn from this? Point out also that Hebrews in the New Testament reviews the Old Testament system, then presents Jesus as superior to that system. Encourage them to read Hebrews in the week to come.

Closing

Reemphasize the importance of worship. Stress that God has always provided a means for people to fellowship with Him. Worship is a privilege never to be taken for granted. Close with prayer.

Assignment

If you chose to use the two exams instead of the final exam, encourage the students to review the material from lessons 1 through 13 in preparation for the exam. Arrange a time to give the exam to the students.

Ask the class members to study Lesson 14 before the next class session. Ask one volunteer to prepare a report about the temple and another to prepare a presentation about the synagogue. Remind the class members to read Hebrews this week.

Variation of Lesson Plan

This week and next week the class could go outdoors, if weather permits, to get a better understanding of the size of the tabernacle and the temple.

Before class, you or the reporter can measure off the distances and place markers on a large open space such as the parking lot or a vacant lot. (The street will serve if necessary.) If you cannot use markers, you might say that the distance is so many parking spaces long, or, from here to the second telephone pole, and so on.

Other markers can be used to show the size of the Holy Place and Most Holy Place. The size of the furniture also can be shown.

Lesson 14—Temple and Synagogue

Attention

As the class members arrive, give each person a sheet of paper and ask him/her to write the word *temple* on the paper with the letters reading vertically down the page. Ask them to make an acrostic by making blank verse, each line beginning with one of the letters, that describes the temple or the activity done there. Here is a sample:

T emple
E xalting God in the
M ost Holy Place
P riests offering sacrifices on the altar
L aver, place of cleansing
E xalting God.

Allow up to ten minutes for this activity. When an individual finishes, have him/her write the verse on a large sheet of newsprint that you have already placed on the wall. Take a few minutes to read these to the class before you proceed with the study section.

Discovery

Begin the study section of this lesson by having the person who prepared the report on the temple make his/her presentation at this time.

Assign the following Scriptures, one to a pair of students. Ask the pair to read it and identify the part(s) of the temple where each event occurred. Allow three to five minutes for them to do this.

1. Luke 1:5-23: Zacharias was burning incense in the Holy Place.
2. Luke 2:21-39: It is likely that Simeon and Anna greeted Jesus in the court of women. But Joseph would have taken the doves into the court of Israel, and the priests would have sacrificed them at the altar in the court of priests.
3. John 2:13-17: The market was in the court of Gentiles.
4. John 10:22, 23: Solomon's porch was on the east side of the court of Gentiles.
5. Mark 12:41-44: The treasury was in the court of women.

6. Acts 3:1-8: The Beautiful Gate was most likely at the east side of the court of women.
7. Acts 21:17-39: Paul was probably seized in the court of women and dragged out into the court of Gentiles. The soldiers rescued him and took him to the Tower of Antonia.

After the groups have finished, call for brief reports and identification of the sites (if shown) on the temple photograph.

Ask for the presentation of the report on the synagogue by the one who prepared it. Be prepared yourself so you can fill in any details.

Now develop a brief discussion around these questions:

1. How was the temple like the tabernacle?
2. How was the temple different from the tabernacle?
3. How was the temple like the church building? Different?
4. How was the synagogue like the church building?
5. How was the synagogue different from the church building?
6. What lessons can we learn from God's careful provision for Old Testament worship?

Closing

Remind the students how very important worship has been and is to God both in the Old Testament era and now. Close with a prayer of praise.

Assignment

Ask the class members to prepare Lesson 15 before class time next week. Encourage them to continue their reading from the Old Testament.

Ask for six volunteers, each to prepare a three- to five-minute report about the six feasts of the Israelites. Encourage them to use a Bible dictionary to assist in preparation.

Lesson 15—The Jewish Feasts

Attention

As the students arrive, ask them to complete the following sentences (which you have displayed on the chalkboard, a transparency, or a poster).
1. When I worship God, I _____.
2. When I think of a feast, I think of _____.
3. When I want to remember something significant, I _____.

Give them four to six minutes to complete these; then have them share their responses with three neighbors for a couple of minutes. Call the groups together and ask: What do these three statements have in common? Develop the discussion around the idea that feasts were times of remembrance and worship in the Old Testament. We sometimes lose that significance in this era.

Discovery

Introduce the Jewish calendar system to the students. In the present system, the Jews celebrate New Year's Day in the fall. But in the Old Testament, the Jewish year began in the spring. Each month had a Hebrew name, although the Bible usually identifies the months by number rather than name. Have volunteers read the references as you talk about each month. Students may copy the calendar into their books.

Now let the students who prepared reports about each of the feasts present their findings. Fill in any essential details that were left unmentioned.

Show how the feasts mentioned in John's Gospel help to date the ministry of Jesus. Ask volunteers to read the following passages.

1. John 2:13-16: It was Passover when Jesus drove the merchants out of the temple.
2. John 5:1-9: This was probably the Passover, for John 4:35 identifies it to be four months until harvest and the other feasts had passed.
3. John 6:1-11: This was Passover time.
4. John 13:1-17: Jesus ate the last supper at Passover.

Since four Passovers are mentioned, we can conclude that Jesus' ministry extended more than three years.

Give a brief lecture on the Day of Atonement. Show how it differed from the six feasts. Point out its significance and procedure.

Feasts in Old Testament times had religious significance. Each feast commemorated a special event in Israel's history. What can we learn from this for our day? How can we use our special days to remind ourselves and our children of our religious heritage? Lead a brief discussion centered on this theme.

Closing

Summarize the content of the last three lessons. If you have time, lead a quick review of these first fifteen lessons, since this concludes the Old Testament survey. Close with prayer.

Assignment

Ask the students to study Lesson 16 prior to the next class session and to answer the questions at the end of the chapter. Encourage them to do the suggested map study and to continue their Bible reading, perhaps adding New Testament reading to their Old Testament meditation this week.

Lesson 16—New Testament Lands

Attention

As each person arrives, give him/her a copy of "Match Them" to complete. Let class members work on this for four or five minutes. Then go over the answers together.

Match Them

B   1. City where Jesus was born.
E   2. Capital of Palestine in Jesus' day.
H   3. Jesus' boyhood home.
A   4. City where Jesus spent much time during His ministry.
F   5. Place where Jesus was baptized.
D   6. Northern province of Palestine.
I   7. Central province of Palestine.
G   8. Southern province of Palestine.
C   9. Southern sea in Palestine.
J   10. Northern sea in Palestine.

Remind the students that all of these places are mentioned often in the New Testament. Our task is to become thoroughly familiar with them.

Discovery

Make copies of the blank maps of Palestine and the New Testament world on pages 64 and 66 in the student book, and give one to each student. (Enlarge maps if possible.) Ask students to fill in sites. Give pertinent facts about the places in Lesson 16: Mediterranean coast, Jordan River, Galilee, Samaria, Judea, Perea, Decapolis, Tetrarchy of Philip, Jerusalem, Bethlehem, Nazareth, and Capernaum. Be sure to prepare carefully, using a Bible dictionary, Bible atlas, and New Testament for resource materials.

Divide your class into groups of two to four and ask each group to do one of the following:

1. Locate the approximate site where a man was beaten by robbers in the parable found in Luke 10:30-36.
2. Find where Jesus fed the five thousand: John 6:1 and Luke 9:10.
3. Estimate the distance from Jerusalem to Bethany. How does that help you understand Matthew 21:17, 18? Estimate the distance from Nazareth to Jerusalem. How long would it take to walk that distance?
4. Locate the places mentioned in Acts 11:26, Acts 28:16, and 1 Corinthians 1:2 and 2 Corinthians 1:1.
5. Trace Paul's first missionary tour, Acts 13:1—14:28.
6. Trace Paul's second missionary tour, Acts 15:35—18:22.
7. Trace Paul's third missionary tour, Acts 18:23—21:15.
8. Trace Paul's voyage to Rome, Acts 27:1—28:16.

Closing

Summarize the session and close with prayer.

Assignments

Urge the students to read Lesson 17 before the next session. Encourage them to continue reading the Bible in their times of meditation. Ask them to make this a review week to make sure they have a grasp on the details of Lessons 1-16.

Lesson 17—The Christ in Prophecy

Attention

Have this incomplete sentence on the chalkboard for the students to answer as they come to the classroom: "When I hear the word *prophecy*, I think of . . ." Ask them to complete the sentence in two or three ways. Then have them join with others to form groups of three and share their answers. Allot five to seven minutes for this. Lead a brief discussion on the meaning of prophecy.

Make the transition into the Bible study section by emphasizing that only the Bible has one hundred percent success in predicting future events. Fortunetellers certainly don't. Nor do politicians, nor do weather forecasters. We know, then, that the Bible is far more than a collection of human wisdom because it is so accurate in foretelling events.

Discovery

The Old Testament foretold the events of Jesus' life with amazing precision. These prophecies were more than the broad details; they extended to specifics. Some were obscure, others clear. Assign the following Scriptures to the students to examine some of the more obscure prophecies.
1. Genesis 3:15—seed of woman shall overcome serpent.
2. Psalm 2:7—quoted in Hebrews 1:5 in reference to Jesus.
3. 2 Samuel 7:14—quoted in Hebrews 1:5 in reference to Jesus.
4. Psalm 45:6, 7—quoted in Hebrews 1:9 in reference to Jesus.
5. Psalm 102:25-27—quoted in Hebrews 1:10-12 in reference to Jesus.
6. Psalm 110:1—quoted in Hebrews 1:13 in reference to Jesus.
7. Psalm 22:22—quoted in Hebrews 2:12 in reference to Jesus.

Those who heard them in the beginning had little, if any, idea of their future fulfillment. They become clear as we look back.

Other prophecies were far more specific. Give students the following matching exercise to do in groups of three or four.

Allot eight to ten minutes for this. Then go over the answers. Identify what prophecy was made and how it was fulfilled.

Match Them		
H	1.	Psalm 22:7, 8
Q	2.	Psalm 22:16
N	3.	Psalm 22:18
O	4.	Psalm 34:20
L	5.	Psalm 41:9
A	6.	Isaiah 9:1, 2
G	7.	Isaiah 53:3
C	8.	Isaiah 53:3
D	9.	Isaiah 53:5, 7
M	10.	Isaiah 53:5
F	11.	Isaiah 53:7
J	12.	Isaiah 53:8
I	13.	Isaiah 53:9
K	14.	Isaiah 53:12
B	15.	Zechariah 9:9
E	16.	Zechariah 11:12, 13
P	17.	Zechariah 12:10

Closing

Reemphasize the uniqueness and divine origin of Bible prophecy. Close with prayer.

Assignment

Ask the students to prepare Lesson 18 before class. Get ten volunteers to present the ten events from Jesus' life. Ask each to confine his/her report to no more than three minutes.

Lesson 18—Life of Christ, Part One

Attention

Distribute the crossword puzzle to the students as they enter the classroom and ask them to complete it.

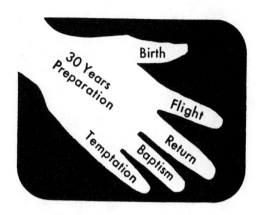

Allot eight to ten minutes for the students to complete this. Then go over the answers with the class. Make the transition into the Bible study by explaining that the events included in the crossword puzzle form the core of today's lesson.

Discovery

Remind students that the memory work in this lesson and the two following ones will be helpful in their Bible study as long as they live.

Review the three periods of New Testament history by filling in a chart like the one on page 70. Help the students memorize the seven separate periods of the life of Christ. Go over this several times. Write the periods on the chalkboard and erase them randomly one at a time as the class names all the periods. Then remind them that this lesson and the next two will present five events from each period of Jesus' life.

Prepare a poster or transparency, or use the chalkboard for a drawing of the hand/fingers drawing.

As the first five students present their reports, print the title of the period on the palm and each event on a finger. Erase those titles and do the same for the second period. (You may trace the hand on blank transparencies to have a hand for each period.) Be sure that no report exceeds three minutes. It may be wise to give them a signal at two minutes. After all the reports are finished, go over them again by using the hand drawing.

Invite reporters to use any of the various maps or charts as they give their reports.

Closing

Use any remaining time to review the content from today. Close with prayer.

Assignment

Ask the class members to prepare Lesson 19 before the next session. Encourage them to continue their Bible reading and also to work on memorization of the facts covered in this lesson. Point out that it will be better to spend a few minutes on this every day, or several times a day, than to study for a long time in one period.

Lesson 19—Life of Christ, Part Two

Attention

Write the following on the chalkboard or on an overhead transparency. As the students arrive, ask them to write a personal response in twenty-five words or less.

Our Bible study today will take us to an important Bible passage. Before we get to it, I want you to respond to the verse just as it is written. Do it in twenty-five words or less. You will have five minutes to do this.

"You are the Christ, the Son of the living God" (Matthew 16:16).

After five minutes, ask the class members to share their responses. Then make the transition into Bible study for today.

Discovery

Review the ten events from the life of Jesus covered last week. Then divide the class into ten groups. Give each group a sheet of newsprint and felt pens. Assign one of the following passages to each group. Ask group members to read the Bible account and draw a picture to depict it.

1. Calling of the fishermen (Matthew 4:18-22).
2. Sermon on the Mount (Matthew 5:1-12).
3. Widow's son (Luke 7:11-17).
4. Lakeside parables (Matthew 13:1-23).
5. Jairus' daughter (Matthew 9:18-26).
6. Feeding of five thousand (Matthew 14:13-21).
7. Syrophoenician's daughter (Matthew 15:21-28).

8. Peter's confession (Matthew 16:13-17).
9. The transfiguration (Matthew 17:1-8).
10. Good Samaritan (Luke 10:29-37).

Allot ten to twelve minutes for this. Then have each group display its picture and give a brief statement of the event.

Closing

Use any remaining time to review the events of this lesson and the last one. Close with prayer.

Seven Periods in Life of Christ

1. Thirty years - preparation
2. First year - obscurity
3. Second year - popularity
4. Third year - opposition
5. Last three months - persecution
6. Last week - passion week
7. Forty days - alive again

Assignment

Ask the class members to prepare Lesson 20 before the next class session. Get one student to volunteer to mark his Bible as suggested on page 79 and be ready to describe the procedure and its merits at the next session. (Allow no more than four minutes for this presentation.) Urge the students to continue work on memorization of the materials covered so far. Encourage them to continue their Bible reading.

Lesson 20—Life of Christ, Part Three

Attention

As the students arrive, give each person the matching exercise. It will serve as a good review of the previous two lessons.

Match Them

G	1. Appearance to Two	F	14. Mary's Anointing
A	2. Baptism	B	15. Nicodemus
A	3. Birth	B	16. Nobleman's Son
C	4. Calling the Fishermen	D	17. Peter's Confession
F	5. Crucifixion	E	18. Rich Young Ruler
D	6. Feeding of Five Thousand	F	19. Ten Virgins
B	7. First Miracle	A	20. Temptation
A	8. Flight	D	21. Transfiguration
D	9. Good Samaritan	F	22. Triumphal Entry
C	10. Jairus' Daughter	F	23. Upper Room
C	11. Lakeside Parables	B	24. Woman of Samaria
E	12. Lazarus	E	25. Zaccheus
E	13. Little Children		

Allow eight to ten minutes for this. Then go over the correct answers.

Make the transition into Bible study by reminding the class that this session considers the last three periods of Jesus' life.

Discovery

Assign one of the following fifteen events to each person (or groups, if there are enough people to make groups). Ask each to write an abridged edition of the assigned section. Each account should be stated in one sentence of fifteen words or less.

1. John 11:1-16—raising of Lazarus.
2. Luke 17:11-19—ten lepers healed.
3. Matthew 19:13-15—little children.
4. Luke 18:18-27—rich young ruler.
5. Luke 19:1-10—Zaccheus.
6. Matthew 26:6-13—Mary's anointing.
7. Matthew 21:1-11—Triumphal entry.
8. Matthew 25:1-13—Ten virgins.
9. Matthew 26:17-29—the upper room.
10. Mark 14:53—15:39—crucifixion.
11. Mark 16:12, 13—appearance to two.
12. Luke 24:36-48—appearance to ten.
13. John 21:1-14—appearance to seven.
14. 1 Corinthians 15:6—appearance to five hundred.
15. Luke 24:36-49—appearance to eleven.

Allot eight to ten minutes for the groups to complete this. Then have each group present its abridged edition of the event.

Have the student who prepared the report on the marked Bible present it at this time.

Closing

Review the three periods in which the New Testament history is divided. Note that we have now finished our study of the first of these three eras. Close with prayer.

Assignment

Ask the class members to prepare Lesson 21 before the next session. Urge them to continue their work on memorization of the details from previous lessons and to begin to memorize Matthew 28:19, 20. Encourage them to continue their Bible reading. Find one volunteer to prepare a five-minute report on "apostle"—what the word means and the qualifications of an apostle. Give him/her a copy of the chart below.

Apostles
Sent
Eyewitnesses
Inspired
Miraculous power

Lesson 21—The Apostles and the Great Commission

Attention

As the students arrive, give each one a copy of the puzzle.

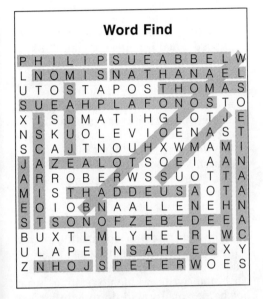

Word Find

Allot eight to ten minutes for the students to complete this puzzle. Then go over the correct answers.

Make the transition into the Bible lesson by stating that the apostles were the appointed successors of Jesus to see that the first-century church was established.

Discovery

Distribute the following passages among the class members: Luke 6:12, 13, 16; Mark 2:13-17; Mark 3:13-19; Matthew 10:2-4; John 1:40-42, 45-49; John 14:22; John 21:2; Acts 1:15-26; Acts 26:15-18. Have each person read his/her verses aloud. In each case, list the names identified on the chalkboard, transparency, or a chart tablet. Refer to the list in the student book on page 80. Explain that, although Canaanite in the Old Testament meant an inhabitant of the land of Canaan, here it refers to a patriotic group that strongly opposed the rule of Rome in Palestine. Zealot is another name for the same.

Teach the song on page 82 to help class

members learn the names of the apostles.

Let the volunteer present the report on apostles. Illustrate the qualifications with Acts 1:21, 22; John 14:26; 16:13; and Matthew 10:1.

Read each of the three Great Commission references. Challenge the students to memorize Matthew 28:19, 20 by next week. Give them the following mnemonic method to help them memorize.

Point out that there are three questions that could be asked about this passage. "Go and do what?" "Doing what?" "And doing what?" Tell them that you will ask a question to which they will answer a part of the verse.

Instructor: "Therefore go and do what?" Students: "Make disciples." Instructor: "Make disciples doing what?" Students: "Baptizing them." Instructor: "And doing what?" Students: "Teaching them."

When they have learned the basic answers to the questions, they simply add the rest of the phrases as they answer the questions. If you have time, you could work through the process with the students. Emphasize the role of each Christian in carrying out the commission.

Closing

Use any remaining time to review the material from the previous New Testament lessons. Close with prayer.

Assignments

Ask students to prepare Lesson 22 before the next class session. Find eight volunteers to prepare reports on each of the following sections from Acts: Acts 2:1-11; Acts 2:12-41; Acts 2:44, 45 & 4:32-37; Acts 5:1-10; Acts 6:1-6; Acts 6:8—7:60; Acts 8:1-4; and Acts 9:1-20. Instruct them to limit their reports to three minutes. Suggest that they use pictures, charts, outlines, or maps. (Direct them to your audiovisual library or children's teachers.)

Lesson 22—Beginnings of the Church

Attention

Prepare several (one for each three or four students) scrambled verses. Use Acts 8:4, "Those who had been scattered preached the word wherever they went" (New International Version). Use 3" x 5" cards, one for each word. Mix these up well and place the cards in an envelope. As the class members arrive, form groups of three or four and give them the envelopes of words. Ask them to make a sensible statement from the words.

Allot five or six minutes for this, if it is needed. Then ask for reports. Lead a brief discussion centered on the students' reactions to the statement. Point out that it is found in Acts, the material for today's lesson.

Discovery

Review the three parts of New Testament history. List them on the chalkboard as the students give them. Include dates. Explain that the beginnings of the church is the topic for today.

Have those who prepared reports present them at this time. Encourage them to use the map to point out where the event of their report happened. Be sure to keep time on the reporters so they do not exceed three minutes. Between reports, fill in any gaps that occur from one report to another.

Carry out the map exercise in the student book, using the New Testament World map. (Or, draw the map from page 85 on chalkboard.) Reemphasize the event(s) associated with each site.

Now divide the class into groups of four or five students. Give each group one, two, or three of the incidents from Acts that were included in the reports of your presentation. Ask each group to reread the sections and then to list any principles for the church today to apply. Allot ten minutes for this. Call for reports. List the suggested principles on the chalkboard. At least the following should be included:

1. The church should grow numerically.
2. Christians care for one another's physical needs.
3. Gross sin must not be tolerated within the church.
4. Organization is acceptable and needed when it helps the church to meet particular needs.
5. Every Christian should feel responsible for spreading the good news.
6. The gospel is for every person everywhere.
7. Missions are at the heart of the church's purpose for existing.
8. The church is to worship and teach to help people grow spiritually.

Lead a brief discussion about how your church rates on application of the principles and how improvement can be made. Ask each person to take a 3" x 5" card and write a memo stating what he/she personally will do to help his/her church carry out the principles.

Closing

Use any remaining time to review the material covered from Lesson 16 through today. Emphasize geography, the life of Christ, as well as the material from the lesson. Then reemphasize the need for the church today to be as much as possible like the church of the first century in function, attitude, and dynamics. Close with prayer.

Assignment

Ask the class to prepare Lesson 23 before the next class session. Remind the members to work on their reviewing in preparation for the final exam or the exam over Lessons 14-26.

Ask for two volunteers each to prepare a five-minute talk, one on baptism and the other on the Lord's Supper. Encourage them to use Bible study helps for their preparation.

Lesson 23—New Life in Christ

Attention

Before time for the students to arrive, place a sheet of newsprint or paper tablecloth on the wall. Use a felt-tip marker to write on it: "A Christian is . . ." Then make available felt-tip markers for each person to write a completion to the sentence as he/she arrives.

After several people have arrived, form groups of three. Ask them to discuss this question: "How am I different this year than I was this time last year?" Allow three to five minutes for this. Then call for reports. You may want to list the responses on the chalkboard.

Tie together these first two activities by pointing out that the implication of the question about change is that it is expected in our lives. The same could have been a completion of "A Christian is . . ." because being a Christian does require continual change. Today's lesson examines some of the changes that occur.

Discovery

Ask the students to turn to 2 Corinthians 5 in their Bibles. Ask them to work in pairs, using nothing but their Bibles, to list ways we become new when we become Christians. Each item listed provides a potential area of growth in the new life. The final list could include these:

1. New hope (vv. 1-3)
2. New strength (v. 4)
3. New purpose (v. 5)
4. New source of power (v. 5)
5. New confidence (v. 6)
6. New sense of direction (v. 7)
7. New standard of approval (v. 9)
8. New motivation (vv. 14, 15)
9. New standard of judgment (v. 16)
10. New reward (vv. 17-19)
11. New work (v. 20)
12. Totally new person (v. 17)

Allot ten minutes for the groups to work, then call for the reports. Spend time discussing what belongs in the list and why.

Then proceed to the two reports on baptism and the Lord's Supper. Be sure to keep time on the reporters so they do not exceed their assigned time limitation. Introduce these by mentioning that baptism is the point where new life begins and that the Lord's Supper provides a week-by-week opportunity to remember again what Christ has done for us.

Now divide the class into groups of six. Assign each group a topic to discuss. Each will begin with, "How would our lives change if we were to apply all of today's principles fully . . ." Give at least one group "at home," another "at work," another "in the community," and another "at church." Allot three to five minutes for the groups to work. Then call for reports, and develop a discussion based on the group responses.

Closing

Take a few minutes to review the New Testament covered thus far in this course.

Then distribute 3" x 5" cards to class members. Ask them to write this sentence (or have it already on the card): "Christ has given me new life. He wants me to grow. I have examined my life, and I commit myself to growth in the following areas." Ask them to write one or two ways in which they will commit themselves to letting God make the necessary changes in their lives in order to experience a totally new life. After they have written their responses, have them form groups of three in which they share their responses. Then have the group members pray together, each person praying for the one on his right.

Assignment

Ask the class members to prepare Lesson 24 before the next class session. Encourage continued review plus pursuit of regular Bible reading.

Get three volunteers to prepare eight- to ten-minute reports, one for each of the three sections in the lesson.

Lesson 24—Life of Paul, Part One

Attention

As the students arrive, give each one a copy of the crossword puzzle. Ask them to complete it.

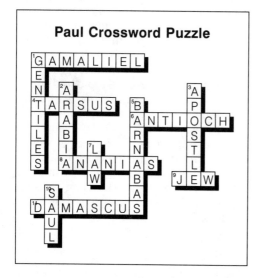

Paul Crossword Puzzle

Allot six to eight minutes for the students to complete this puzzle. Go over the correct answers. Then explain that Paul's early life forms the content for today's lesson.

Discovery

Point out that the life of Paul can be divided into six periods. Today's lesson covers the first three periods.
Saul, the student
Saul, the persecutor
Saul, the convert

Paul, the missionary
Paul, the author
Paul, the martyr
Now have the three people who prepared presentations make their reports. Be sure to fill in any omitted details.

After the reports, do the map exercise on page 91 of the student book, using a map that you have drawn on the chalkboard or traced onto a transparency.

Identify Tarsus, Damascus, Jerusalem, and Antioch.

Closing

Use any extra time for review of the New Testament material from Lesson 16 through today. Emphasize the six periods of Paul's life. Then quickly review the details of this lesson. Close with prayer.

Assignment

Ask the class members to prepare Lesson 25 before the next class session. Encourage them to read Acts 13—28 which discloses the details of Paul's missionary travels.

Get four volunteers to prepare five- to eight-minute reports on the three missionary journeys of Paul plus his trip to Rome. Encourage them to prepare carefully, using the Bible material as the major basis for the reports.

Remind the students to work on reviewing the lessons in this study so they will be prepared for the final exam or the exam over lessons 14 through 26.

Lesson 25—Life of Paul, Part Two

Attention

As the students arrive, ask them to prepare an acrostic, using a word or phrase for each letter that is associated with "Missionary." A sample completed acrostic is included below.

Missionary Acrostic

M y responsibility
I nternational
S ent
S pread good news
I nto all the world
O verseas
N earby
A t home
R edemption
Y our responsibility

Allot six to eight minutes for this. Then fill out a master acrostic on an overhead transparency or a chart, allowing each contributor to explain why he/she included what he/she did.

Discovery

Review the three periods of New Testament history as well as the six periods of Paul's life. Then explain that this lesson covers the final three periods of Paul's life.

Have the four reporters who prepared presentations regarding Paul's three missionary journeys plus his voyage to Rome give their reports at this time. Keep them within the assigned time limits.

Briefly present the material on Paul the martyr and the later work of John. Include information about John's books of the New Testament. Remind students that dates given are approximate. We can be sure of the facts given in the Bible, and the dates we have are near enough to give a general idea of the time involved.

Closing

Use any remaining time to review the material from the New Testament lessons. Then close with prayer.

Assignment

Ask the class members to prepare Lesson 26 prior to the next class session. Urge them to work on reviewing the entire series of lessons. Also encourage them to continue their Bible reading.

Ask for five volunteers to prepare these presentations: 1) "The Divine Purpose" in the lesson, 2) "Missionary Examples" in the lesson, 3) a world map with countries marked where missionary activity is being conducted, 4) a listing of areas not yet reached by the gospel, and 5) a report on your church's mission program. Give them a five-minute limit for each presentation.

Lesson 26—The Bible for the Whole World

Attention

As the students arrive, give them a copy of the review.

Allot eight to ten minutes for this. Then go over the correct answers.

Explain that today's lesson, the last in this study, will examine the work the church has yet to do.

Discovery

Display a world map or a globe. Point to the world and explain that the world is the basis for the work of the church.

Then ask the five speakers to present the material they prepared for today. Keep the reports within the assigned five-minute guidelines. Be prepared to fill in any omitted material.

Closing

Use the remaining minutes to answer questions about and/or to review the material covered during these six months. Close with prayer.

Assignment

Encourage the students to review the material from the entire course in preparation for the final exam, or from lessons 14 through 26 if taking the exam only over those lessons. Urge them to continue in their regular Bible reading program.

Review

PEOPLE
H   1. Apostle who denied Jesus
B   2. Disciple who told Peter about Jesus
A   3. Father of the Israelites
F   4. Leader of the Israelites
C   5. Old Testament prophet
I   6. Preached to the Ethiopian
D   7. Old Testament judge
E   8. Son of Jacob
G   9. Early missionary
J   10. Third king of Israel

BOOK
G   1. Rebuilding of Jerusalem
B   2. Crossing of the Red Sea
J   3. New Testament letter
A   4. Tells of Paul's mission work
H   5. Book of poetry
E   6. Settling Canaan
C   7. Creation of man
I   8. Last book of the Bible
F   9. One of the Gospels
D   10. Book of prophecy

PLACE
F   1. God gave the Ten Commandments
E   2. Where Elijah prayed for fire
C   3. Capital of Judah
I   4. Paul was imprisoned here
J   5. Abraham's original home
A   6. Place where Jesus was born
B   7. Where Jesus was taken as a young child
D   8. Where Jesus was baptized
H   9. The Israelites crossed it
G   10. Jesus' hometown

Worksheet for Philemon

1. Read the entire book of Philemon.

2. Who wrote the book of Philemon?

3. To whom was Philemon written?

4. Write the key words in the text.

5. Develop a brief outline of the book.

6. Write a one-sentence summary for each section of the outline.

7. Summarize the problem addressed in the book.

8. What was the intended meaning of verses 17-21?

9. What principles for living today does this book present?

[33]

Match Them

1. Collection of 39 books.

2. Five books of law.

3. Four gospels.

4. One book of prophecy.

5. Five books of poetry.

6. Twenty-one letters.

7. Collection of 27 books.

8. Seventeen books of prophecy.

9. One book of history.

10. Twelve books of history.

_____ **Old Testament**

_____ **New Testament**

The Old Testament Books

You can find the names of all of the books of the Old Testament in the puzzle below. The names go across, backward, forward, up, and down.

```
A D E C C L E S I A S T E S U W P
H A X T H U H A I M E H E N R L R
A N O V O H A G B N A H U M I K O
I I D B S J E J U D G E S S A V
D E U T E R O N O M Y E Z R A S E
A L S O A M N E B U H A C I M S R
B J O S H U A S A C H R O N U E B
O H A B B A H I M R E H T S E L S
E L P S A L M S O Z O J O E L C K
L E V I T I C U S O X W Y R L I U
K I O S N O G U S R E B M U N N K
I K N A Z E C H A R I A H T W O K
N E L I H A I N A H P E Z H O R A
G N Z L A M E N T A T I O N S O H B
S E O H A G G A I Y Z N O T S C A
H A I M E R E J M A L A C H I A H
E G C N O M O L O S F O G N O S B
```

Match Them

Match each place below with its proper identification.

——— 1. Tigris
——— 2. Egypt
——— 3. Ararat
——— 4. Babylonia
——— 5. Nebo
——— 6. Red Sea
——— 7. Great Sea
——— 8. Assyria
——— 9. Israel
——— 10. Sinai
——— 11. Euphrates
——— 12. Nile
——— 13. Persia
——— 14. Carmel
——— 15. Jordan

A. Body of Water
B. Empire
C. Mountain
D. River

Lesson 5

New Testament Books Crossword

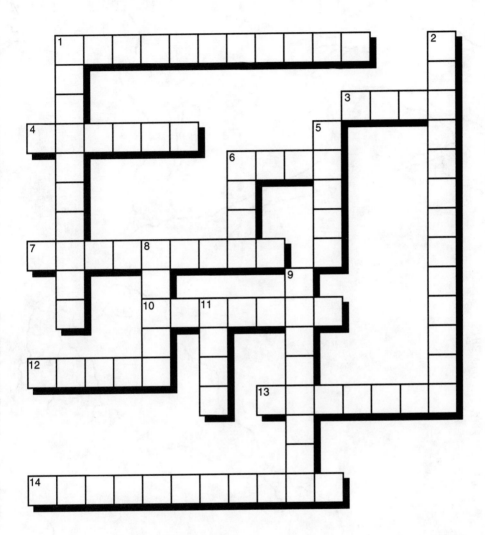

Across

1. Paul wrote two letters to these Christians.
3. Third Gospel.
4. Found after Acts.
6. This writer was a brother of James.
7. Found before Ephesians.
10. Paul wrote two letters to this young man.
12. Practical letter found after Hebrews.
13. Found after Philemon.
14. Letter of joy.

Down

1. Found after Philippians.
2. Two letters written by Paul.
5. Two letters found after James.
6. Four books carry his name.
8. Found before Hebrews.
9. Book Paul wrote about a slave who became a Christian.
11. Second Gospel.

Lesson 7

THE OLD TESTAMENT WORLD

Find Them

Find the names of the sixteen major Old Testament characters. They may be found horizontally, vertically, diagonally, backward, or forward.

```
N G A M A D A J O S J U
O I B U L O N O A H O N
M D R O D A N I A L S U
O E A L A N O J S S E T
L O H A N D I V A D P H
O N A B I L T U O A H A
S A M U E L L T O M N I
O L E M L M O S E S U A
J E R E M I A H J U M S
H A I M E H E N G E N I
W A L T A U H S O J S A
```

Match Them

_____ 1. Abraham
_____ 2. Adam
_____ 3. Daniel
_____ 4. David
_____ 5. Elijah
_____ 6. Ezra
_____ 7. Gideon
_____ 8. Isaiah
_____ 9. Jeremiah
_____ 10. Joseph
_____ 11. Joshua
_____ 12. Malachi
_____ 13. Moses
_____ 14. Nehemiah
_____ 15. Noah
_____ 16. Samuel
_____ 17. Saul
_____ 18. Solomon

A. Conquest
B. Decline
C. Power
D. Preparation
E. Probation
F. Servitude

Lesson 10

Review Acrostic

1. _ _ _ _ _ _ _ _   Old Testament book following Amos.

2. _ _ _ _ _ _ _ _   Third section of New Testament books.

3. _ _ _ _ _ _ _ _   Fifth period of Old Testament history.

4. _ _ _ _ _ _ _   Prominent river in the Old Testament.

5. _ _ _ _ _   Old Testament book of history.

6. _ _ _ _ _ _ _   Major Old Testament character.

7. _ _ _ _ _ _ _   Two New Testament letters bear this name.

8. _ _ _ _ _ _ _ _   Old Testament empire.

9. _ _ _ _ _ _ _ _ _ _ _ _   Important Old Testament area.

10. _ _ _ _ _ _ _   Old Testament book.

11. _ _ _ _ _ _ _ _   Major Old Testament character.

12. _ _ _ _ _ _ _ _ _ _ _ _ _   Two New Testament letters bear this name.

13. _ _ _ _ _ _ _ _ _   First period of Old Testament history.

14. _ _ _ _ _ _   Old Testament empire.

15. _ _ _ _ _ _ _ _ _ _   Promise given in Genesis 3.

16. _ _ _ _ _ _ _   Major Old Testament character.

17. _ _ _   _ _ _ _ _ _ _ _   One of the two divisions of the Bible.

18. _ _ _ _ _ _   Old Testament book of prophecy.

19. _ _ _ _ _ _ _ _ _   Sixth period of Old Testament history.

Match Them

1. City where Jesus was born.

2. Capital of Palestine in Jesus' day.

3. Jesus' boyhood home.

4. City where Jesus spent much time during His ministry.

5. Place where Jesus was baptized.

6. Northern province of Palestine.

7. Central province of Palestine.

8. Southern province of Palestine.

9. Southern sea in Palestine.

10. Northern sea in Palestine.

A. Capernaum
B. Bethlehem
C. Dead Sea
D. Galilee
E. Jerusalem
F. Jordan River
G. Judea
H. Nazareth
I. Samaria
J. Sea of Galilee

Match Them

Match the New Testament fulfillment with the Old Testament prophecy. Use your Bible to help you.

1. Psalm 22:7, 8

2. Psalm 22:16

3. Psalm 22:18

4. Psalm 34:20

5. Psalm 41:9

6. Isaiah 9:1, 2

7. Isaiah 53:3

8. Isaiah 53:3

9. Isaiah 53:5, 7

10. Isaiah 53:5

11. Isaiah 53:7

12. Isaiah 53:8

13. Isaiah 53:9

14. Isaiah 53:12

15. Zechariah 9:9

16. Zechariah 11:12, 13

17. Zechariah 12:10

A. Matthew 4:12-16
B. Matthew 21:4, 5
C. Matthew 26:36-38
D. Matthew 26:67, 68; 27:27-30
E. Matthew 27:3-10
F. Matthew 27:12-14
G. Matthew 27:21-23
H. Matthew 27:41-43
I. Matthew 27:57-60
J. Mark 14:61-64; 15:15
K. Mark 15:27, 28
L. John 13:18
M. John 19:1
N. John 19:23, 24
O. John 19:36
P. John 19:37
Q. John 20:20, 25, 27

Life of Jesus Crossword

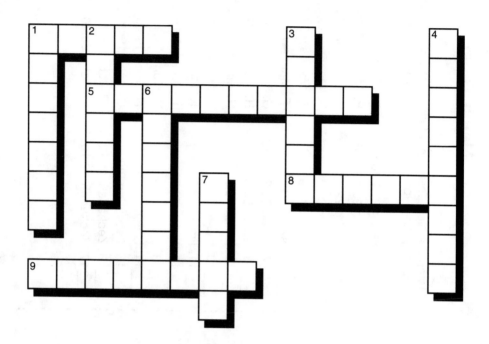

Across

1. Luke 2:1-20 records the _____ of Jesus.
5. Matthew 4:1-11 records the _____ of Jesus.
8. Jesus cleansed the _____ in John 2:13-16.
9. Jesus healed the son of a _____ in John 4:46-54.

Down

1. Matthew 3:13-17 records Jesus' _____.
2. Matthew 2:19-23 tells about the _____from Egypt.
3. Matthew 2:1-15 tells about the _____ to Egypt.
4. _____ came to Jesus at night (John 3:1-21).
6. Jesus' first _____ was performed in Cana of Galilee (John 2:1-11).
7. Jesus revealed who He was first to a _____ in Samaria (John 4:1-21).

Match Them

Match each event from the life of Jesus with the proper period.

EVENT

___ 1. Appearance to Two
___ 2. Baptism
___ 3. Birth
___ 4. Calling the Fishermen
___ 5. Crucifixion
___ 6. Feeding of Five Thousand
___ 7. First Miracle
___ 8. Flight
___ 9. Good Samaritan
___ 10. Jairus' Daughter
___ 11. Lakeside Parables
___ 12. Lazarus
___ 13. Little Children
___ 14. Mary's Anointing
___ 15. Nicodemus
___ 16. Nobleman's Son
___ 17. Peter's Confession
___ 18. Rich Young Ruler
___ 19. Ten Virgins
___ 20. Temptation

___ 21. Transfiguration
___ 22. Triumphal Entry
___ 23. Upper Room
___ 24. Woman of Samaria
___ 25. Zaccheus

PERIOD

A. Preparation
B. Obscurity
C. Popularity
D. Opposition
E. Persecution
F. Passion Week
G. Alive Again

Word Find

Jesus had twelve apostles. Some of them had two names. Find the names of the twelve, plus names associated with them, in the puzzle below. You may go backward, forward, up, down, or diagonally.

```
P H I L I P S U E A B B E L W
L N O M I S N A T H A N A E L
U T O S T A P O S T H O M A S
S U E A H P L A F O N O S T O
X I S D M A T I H G L O T J E
N S K U O L E V I O E N A S T
S C A J T N O U H X W M A M I
J A Z E A L O T S O E I A A N
A R R O B E R W S S U O T T A
M I S T H A D D E U S A O T A
E O I O B N A A L L E N E H N
S T S O N O F Z E B E D E E A
B U X T L M L Y H E L R L W C
U L A P E I N S A H P E C X Y
Z N H O J S P E T E R W O E S
```

Paul Crossword Puzzle

Across

1. Paul's teacher (Acts 22:3).
4. Paul's birthplace (Acts 22:3).
6. Where Paul went to work with Barnabas (Acts 13:1).
8. The man who baptized Paul (Acts 9:17, 18).
9. Paul's nationality (Acts 22:3).
11. The city near which Paul received a vision (Acts 9:3).

Down

1. Paul was the apostle to the _____ (Acts 22:21).
2. Paul first went to _____ after his conversion (Galatians 1:17).
3. Paul was an _____ (Galatians 1:1).
5. The one who introduced Paul to the other apostles in Jerusalem (Acts 9:27).
7. What Paul studied (Acts 22:3).
10. Paul's name before he became a Christian (Acts 8:1).

Lesson 26

Review!

Match the correct name, place, or book with the description on the left.

PEOPLE

___ 1. Apostle who denied Jesus
___ 2. Disciple who told Peter about Jesus
___ 3. Father of the Israelites
___ 4. Leader of the Israelites
___ 5. Old Testament prophet
___ 6. Preached to the Ethiopian
___ 7. Old Testament judge
___ 8. Son of Jacob
___ 9. Early missionary
___ 10. Third king of Israel

A. Abraham
B. Andrew
C. Elijah
D. Gideon
E. Joseph
F. Moses
G. Paul
H. Peter
I. Philip
J. Solomon

PLACE

___ 1. God gave the Ten Commandments
___ 2. Where Elijah prayed for fire
___ 3. Capital of Judah
___ 4. Paul was imprisoned here
___ 5. Abraham's original home
___ 6. Place where Jesus was born
___ 7. Where Jesus was taken as a young child
___ 8. Where Jesus was baptized
___ 9. The Israelites crossed it
___ 10. Jesus' hometown

A. Bethlehem
B. Egypt
C. Jerusalem
D. Jordan River
E. Mount Carmel
F. Mount Sinai
G. Nazareth
H. Red Sea
I. Rome
J. Ur

BOOK

___ 1. Rebuilding of Jerusalem
___ 2. Crossing of the Red Sea
___ 3. New Testament letter
___ 4. Tells of Paul's mission work
___ 5. Book of poetry
___ 6. Settling Canaan
___ 7. Creation of man
___ 8. Last book of the Bible
___ 9. One of the Gospels
___ 10. Book of prophecy

A. Acts
B. Exodus
C. Genesis
D. Isaiah
E. Joshua
F. Mark
G. Nehemiah
H. Psalms
I. Revelation
J. Romans

Exam on Lessons 1 through 13

1. About how many human writers produced parts of the Bible?
2. How do you account for the complete harmony of these different parts that were produced by different writers at different times?
3. In what languages was the Bible originally written?
4. What can you tell about the ancient manuscripts and versions from which our Bible was translated?
5. Give two purposes of Bible study.
6. Name the divisions of the Old Testament and give the number of books in each division.
7. Name the books in the first two divisions of the Old Testament.
8. Name the books in the last two divisions of the Old Testament.
9. Name the divisions of the New Testament and give the number of books in each division.
10. Give the purpose of each group of New Testament books.
11. Name the books in the last two divisions of the New Testament.
12. What is a dispensation?
13. Name three great dispensations.
14. Draw from memory a rough outline map of the Old Testament world.
15. Write the names of three important areas on your map.
16. Write the names of four rivers on your map.
17. Write the names of three bodies of water on your map.
18. Name sixteen leading Old Testament characters.
19. Name six periods of Old Testament history.
20. In the list of characters written for question 18, draw lines to divide the list into sections corresponding to the six periods.
21. List seven epochs of the final period of Old Testament history.
22. For what were altars used?
23. Why was the tabernacle a portable building rather than a permanent one?
24. What articles of furniture were in the court of the tabernacle?
25. What articles of furniture were in the Holy Place and the Most Holy Place?

Exam on Lessons 14 through 26

1. What three men directed the building of temples for Israel at different times?
2. Which of the temples was standing when Jesus was on earth as a man?
3. Name the three great feasts of the Jews.
4. What event was commemorated by the Passover feast?
5. Mention an event of New Testament times that occurred at the time of a feast.
6. What great feast was on only one day each year? How long were the others?
7. Name three lesser feasts of the Jews.
8. In Jesus' time, what three main divisions of Palestine lay west of the Jordan River?
9. What three divisions lay east of the Jordan River?
10. Name the town where Jesus was born, the town where He lived as a youth, the town often called His headquarters during His ministry, and the town where He was crucified.
11. Sketch a crude outline map of the lands where Paul traveled.
12. On your map, mark the cities of Jerusalem, Antioch, Philippi, Corinth, and Rome.
13. Mention five details of Christ's life that were foretold by Old Testament prophets.
14. Why were the prophecies about Jesus not understood by the scholars of Jesus' time?
15. List seven periods in the life of Christ.
16. List five events of the middle period of the seven.
17. What does the word "apostle" mean? Why were Jesus' apostles given that name?
18. Name the twelve apostles.
19. What other men are called apostles in the New Testament?
20. What is the great commission?
21. When the apostles began to preach the gospel on Pentecost, how could people tell that the Holy Spirit was with them?
22. Name some of the new things that appear in a person's life when he/she becomes a new creature in Christ.
23. List six periods in the life of Paul.
24. Briefly tell what happened in one of these periods—any one you choose.
25. Tell a little about what has been done to take the Bible to the whole world.

Answers to Exam on Lessons 1-13

1. 40.
2. Inspired by God.
3. Hebrew and Greek.
4. Manuscripts were written by hand. Versions are translations.
5. To know God. To guide our lives.
6. Law—5, History—12, Poetry—5, Prophecy—17.
7. Genesis, Exodus, Leviticus, Numbers, Deuteronomy; Joshua, Judges, Ruth, 1 & 2 Samuel, 1 & 2 Kings, 1 & 2 Chronicles, Ezra, Nehemiah, Esther.
8. Job, Psalms, Proverbs, Ecclesiastes, Song of Solomon; Isaiah, Jeremiah, Lamentations, Ezekiel, Daniel, Hosea, Joel, Amos, Obadiah, Jonah, Micah, Nahum, Habakkuk, Zephaniah, Haggai, Zechariah, Malachi.
9. Gospels—4, History—1, Letters—21, Prophecy—1.
10. Gospels—to lead us to know Jesus is the Christ, Son of God. History—to show people today how to become Christians and carry on the work of the church. Letters—to guide Christians in their living, helping them to obey what Jesus commanded. Prophecy—tells of the final victory of Christ and his people. To encourage us to keep on living as Christians should.
11. Romans, 1 & 2 Corinthians, Galatians, Ephesians, Philippians, Colossians, 1 & 2 Thessalonians, 1 & 2 Timothy, Titus, Philemon, Hebrews, James, 1 & 2 Peter, 1, 2, & 3 John, Jude; Revelation.
12. A plan by which God dispenses or gives out His revelation, blessing, or punishment.
13. Patriarchal, Jewish or Mosaic, Christian.
14. See map in student book.
15. See map in student book.
16. See map in student book.
17. See map in student book.
18. [Adam, Noah], [Abraham, Joseph], [Moses, Joshua, Gideon, Samuel], [Saul, David, Solomon], [Elijah, Isaiah, Jeremiah], [Daniel, Nehemiah].
19. Probation, Preparation, Conquest, Power, Decline, Servitude.
20. See brackets in 18.
21. Babylonian rule, Persian, Greek, Syrian, Egyptian, Maccabean Freedom, Roman.
22. Altars were used for sacrifices to seek forgiveness, offer thanksgiving, etc.
23. It permitted people to transport their place of worship with them when traveling.
24. Altar of burnt offering and laver.
25. Table of Shewbread, candlestick, Altar of Incense, Veil, Ark of Covenant.

Answers to Exam on Lessons 14-26

1. Solomon, Zerubbabel, Herod.
2. Herod's.
3. Passover, Pentecost, Tabernacles.
4. Passing over of death to first-born in Egypt.
5. Passover—Jesus teaching in temple as a child, Jesus' crucifixion. Pentecost—Beginning of the church, Peter's sermon, giving of the Holy Spirit.
6. Pentecost. One week.
7. Trumpets, Purim, Dedication.
8. Judea, Samaria, Galilee.
9. Perea, Decapolis, Tetrarchy of Philip.
10. Bethlehem, Nazareth, Capernaum, Jerusalem.
11-12. See map in student book.
13. Minister in Galilee, enter Jerusalem in triumph, despised and rejected, man of sorrows, betrayed by a friend, price of thirty pieces of silver, silent while on trial, sentenced to death, suffer abuse, scourged, hands and feet pierced, garments shared by lots, numbered with transgressors, endured cruel mockery, no bone was to be broken, He was to be pierced (side), with the rich in death, born in Bethlehem, born of a virgin.
14. Obscure prophecies (not understood until fulfilled). Time element (no distinction between first and second coming). Selfish wishes (Jews only wanted the glory, not the suffering).
15. Thirty years—preparation. First year—obscurity. Second year—popularity. Third year—opposition. Last three months—persecution. Last week—passion week. Forty days—alive again.
16. Feeding of the five thousand. Syrophoenician's daughter. Peter's confession. Transfiguration. Good Samaritan.
17. One who is sent. Because they were sent into the world to preach the gospel.
18. Simon (Peter), Andrew, James, John, Philip, Bartholomew, Thomas, Matthew, James, Thaddaeus, Simon, Judas Iscariot.
19. Paul and Matthias.
20. Matthew 28:19, 20. (See Bible.)
21. Spoke in tongues.
22. Standard, hope, outlook, incentive, purpose, reward, duties, obligations, behavior.
23. Student, persecutor, convert, missionary, author, martyr.
24. Student—studies under Gamaliel. Persecutor—was present at Stephen's stoning. Convert—incidents on road to Damascus. Missionary—traveled in Asia Minor, Greece, to Rome. Author—wrote about half of the books of the New Testament. Martyr—probably put to death during Nero's persecutions.
25. Missionaries; Bible translations into other languages; TV and radio broadcasts; Christian literature sent to other countries.

Final Exam

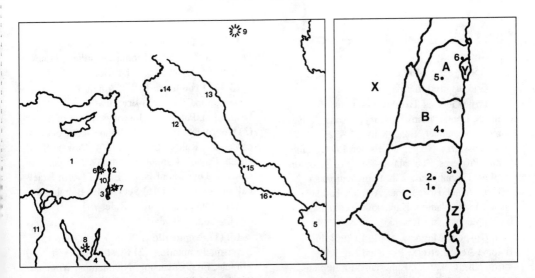

1. Why do we regard the Bible as our authority in worship and life?
2. About how many people wrote parts of the Bible?
3. About how much time passed between the writing of the first book and the writing of the last?
4. How can we account for the remarkable harmony of all the books?
5. Name four divisions of the Old Testament and list the books in each.
6. Name four divisions of the New Testament and list the books in each.
7. Name the seas, mountains, rivers, and cities numbered on the first map above.
8. Name the three areas marked with the letters A, B, and C on the second map.
9. Name the numbered towns that are associated with Jesus.
10. Name the seas marked X, Y, Z.
11. Name sixteen Old Testament people and tell who each one was or what he did.
12. Name Jesus' twelve apostles.
13. Name six periods of Old Testament history and list three events in each.
14. About how much time passed between the end of the Old Testament and the beginning of the New?
15. Name seven periods of the life of Christ and list five events in each.
16. On Pentecost when the church began to grow, who preached the sermon that is recorded?
17. How many people became followers of Christ on that day?
18. What made many members of the church leave Jerusalem?
19. What evangelist took the gospel to Samaria and to a traveler leaving Jerusalem?
20. What apostle first took the gospel to Gentiles? Name a notable man among the first Gentile converts.
21. What enemy of the church later became famous for preaching to Gentiles?
22. Name five or more cities where that former enemy preached during his three missionary journeys.
23. In what capital city was the great missionary to Gentiles imprisoned twice?
24. To which of the cities (question 22) did the missionary write letters that are included in the Bible?
25. Tell a little about what has been done to take the Bible to the whole world.

Answers for Final Exam

1. Because it is the inspired Word of God.
2. About forty.
3. 1,500 years: 1400 B.C. to A.D. 100.
4. God inspired them all.
5. **Law:** Genesis, Exodus, Leviticus, Numbers, Deuteronomy. **History:** Joshua, Judges, Ruth, 1 & 2 Samuel, 1 & 2 Kings, 1 & 2 Chronicles, Ezra, Nehemiah, Esther. **Poetry:** Job, Psalms, Proverbs, Ecclesiastes, Song of Solomon. **Prophecy:** Isaiah, Jeremiah, Lamentations, Ezekiel, Daniel, Hosea, Joel, Amos, Obadiah, Jonah, Micah, Nahum, Habakkuk, Zephaniah, Haggai, Zechariah, Malachi.
6. **Gospels:** Matthew, Mark, Luke, John. **History:** Acts. **Letters:** Romans, 1 & 2 Corinthians, Galatians, Ephesians, Philippians, Colossians, 1 & 2 Thessalonians, 1 & 2 Timothy, Titus, Philemon, Hebrews, James, 1 & 2 Peter, 1, 2, & 3 John, Jude. **Prophecy:** Revelation.
7. **Seas:** (1) Great (Mediterranean), (2) Galilee (Gennesaret), (3) Dead (Salt), (4) Red, (5) Persian Gulf. **Mountains:** (6) Carmel, (7) Nebo, (8) Sinai, (9) Ararat. **Rivers:** (10) Jordan, (11) Nile, (12) Euphrates, (13) Tigris. **Cities:** (14) Haran, (15) Babylon, (16) Ur.
8. (A) Galilee, (B) Samaria, (C) Judea.
9. (1) Bethlehem, (2) Jerusalem, (3) Jericho, (4) Sychar, (5) Nazareth, (6) Capernaum.
10. (X) Great (now called Mediterranean), (Y) Galilee (also called Gennesaret), (Z) Dead Sea (also called Salt Sea).
11. (1) **Adam**, the first man. (2) **Noah** built ark, survived flood. (3) **Abraham**, father of Jewish people. (4) **Joseph**, Jewish ruler in Egypt. (5) **Moses** led Israel out of Egypt. (6) **Joshua** led fight for promised land. (7) **Gideon**, one of many judges. (8) **Samuel**, judge and prophet. (9) **Saul**, first king of Israel. (10) **David**, warrior, king, musician. (11) **Solomon**, wisest king of Israel. (12) **Elijah**, prophet in north Israel. (13) **Isaiah**, prophet in south Israel. (14) **Jeremiah**, prophet in south Israel. (15) **Daniel**, prophet in Babylon. (16) **Nehemiah** rebuilt Jerusalem. (These are listed in *Training for Service*. Give credit if other Old Testament people are named instead.)

12. Simon (Peter), Andrew, James, John, Philip, Bartholomew, Thomas, Matthew, James, Thaddaeus, Simon, Judas Iscariot.
13. (1) **Probation:** Fall of Adam, Promise of Redemption, Flood. (2) **Preparation:** Dispersion, Patriarchs' Journeys, Israel in Egypt. (3) **Conquest:** Wilderness Wandering, Conquest of Canaan, Rule of the Judges. (4) **Power:** Saul's Death, David's Capital, Solomon's Temple. (5) **Decline:** Division of Israel, End of North Israel, Fall of South Israel. (6) **Servitude:** Babylonian Rule, Persian Rule, Greek Rule.
14. About 400 years.
15. (1) **Preparation:** Birth, Flight, Return, Baptism, Temptation. (2) **First Year:** First Miracle, First Cleansing, Nicodemus, Woman of Samaria, Nobleman's Son. (3) **Second Year:** Calling Fishers, Sermon on the Mount, Widow's Son, Lakeside Parables, Jairus' Daughter. (4) **Third Year:** Feeding Five Thousand, Syrophoenician's Daughter, Peter's Confession, Transfiguration, Good Samaritan. (5) **Last Three Months:** Raising of Lazarus, Ten Lepers Healed, Little Children, Rich Young Ruler, Zaccheus. (6) **Last Week:** Anointing by Mary, Triumphal Entry, Ten Virgins, Upper Room, Crucifixion. (7) **Forty Days:** Appearance to Two, Appearance to Ten, Appearance to Seven, Appearance to Five Hundred, Appearance to Eleven.
16. Simon Peter.
17. Three thousand.
18. Persecution.
19. Philip.
20. Simon Peter; Cornelius.
21. Saul, later called Paul.
22. Salamis, Paphos, Antioch, Iconium, Derbe, Lystra, Philippi, Thessalonians, Berea, Athens, Corinth, Ephesus.
23. Rome.
24. Rome, Corinth, Ephesus, Philippi, Thessalonica.
25. Missionaries; Bible translations into other languages; TV and radio broadcasts; Christian literature sent to other countries.

A SURVEY OF THE BIBLE

Training for Service

STUDENT BOOK

by ORRIN ROOT

Revised By Eleanor Daniel

STANDARD
PUBLISHING
Cincinnati, Ohio

Library of Congress Cataloging in Publication Data

Root, Orrin.
   Training for service.

   At head of title: Student.
   Summary: A survey of the contents of the Bible including historical sidelights and study questions.
   1. Bible—Textbooks.   2. Bible—Criticism, interpretation, etc. [1. Bible—study] I. Daniel, Eleanor
Ann. II. Title.
[BS605.2.R67 1983]   220.6'1   83-4678
ISBN 0-87239-704-1

06 05 04 03   22 21

Foreword

Herbert Moninger's original *Training for Service* was published in 1907 and immediately became a favorite text for the training of Sunday school teachers. After being reprinted many times with minor changes, it was thoroughly revised by C. J. Sharp in 1934. It then received the title, *New Training for Service*, and continued to be reprinted with minor changes from time to time. Through all its editions the book retained its popularity, and over a long period an average of twenty-five thousand copies a year went out to eager students.

In response to a multitude of requests for a shorter and more specialized study, we offered another complete revision of this ever-popular work. Moninger's original plan of Bible study was retained, but now there were twenty-six lessons instead of forty. This was accomplished by omitting the study of principles and methods of teaching and some lessons on Christian evidences, which were offered more fully in other books in Standard's training courses.

Training for Service thus became more specifically a survey of the Bible, a basic need of every Sunday school teacher. It helped teachers gain a comprehensive knowledge of the Bible as a whole. This knowledge is a setting in which any part of the Scripture becomes more meaningful, a background that makes each Bible lesson easier and more rewarding.

Training for Service—A Survey of the Bible became very popular with church leaders as a basic course for new Christians. More and more Christians were helped in their Bible study.

Now we respond to those who requested that we update the information in the book, but not change its essence. That has been done in this revision. Suggestions have been added to the lesson plans in the instructor's edition, and reproducible worksheets have been included to make the teaching more effective. In the student edition we have added a pronunciation guide, updated the information on Bible translations, added a history of the period between the testaments, and given the book a new look. *Training for Service—A Survey of the Bible* should continue to be one of the best teaching tools that the local church can use.

CONTENTS

TIPS FOR STUDY

Training for Service—A Survey of the Bible has proved to be immensely popular among church leaders since its publication in 1907. It appeals to thousands of earnest Christians who are enthusiastic about the help it gives them in their Bible study.

Student Participation

It is assumed that each student will study carefully and come to class ready to recite the facts of the lesson and join in the discussion of them. In addition, you should carefully accept special assignments and do your part in any way the leader asks.

Memorization and Review

The place of memory work in education is much smaller than it used to be. It is still necessary to learn the alphabet, however, for without it one can hardly use a dictionary or a telephone directory.

For similar reasons, you will learn the names of the books of the Bible in order so that you can quickly find a passage when you want it. When you have learned to name the leading Bible characters in order, you will ever after know that Moses comes later than Joseph and earlier than David. This book has many other lists to be memorized. They are the ABC's of Bible study. It will not take long to learn them, and they will be a lifelong help in studying the Scripture.

Bible References

Every Christian should be able to find any passage of Scripture quickly and read it aloud intelligently and with expression. You will gain experience in finding and reading Bible texts as Scripture references are used in class. In most lessons you should look up and read all the references given. When a passage is very long, you may be asked to study it in advance and give the class a brief summary. When there are many such references, the teacher may decide who will read which references.

Equipment

You will need a Bible and your own copy of *Training for Service—A Survey of the Bible*. A Bible dictionary, a Bible concordance, and an English dictionary will be helpful.

Independent Study

If a *Training for Service* class is not available, an individual may complete this course as an independent study. That person must choose a teacher, minister, or other qualified person to administer the final exam and grade it. The chosen person will sign and present a certificate to the student who has received a grade of 70% or more on the final exam. That person must request the exam and the certificate from Standard Publishing, c/o Christian Ministries Department, 8121 Hamilton Ave., Cincinnati, OH 45231.

Pronunciation Guide

AARON   *Air*-un
AB   Ahv
ABEL   *Aye*-buhl
ABIAH   Uh-*bye*-uh
ABIB   Ah-*veev*
ABNER   *Ab*-ner
ABRAHAM   *Aye*-bruh-ham
ABSALOM   *Ab*-suh-lum
ADAM   *A*-dum
ADAR   Ah-*dar*
AHAB   *Aye*-hab
ALEXANDER   Al-ex-*an*-der
ALPHEUS   Al-*fee*-us
AMOS   *Aye*-mus
ANANIAS   An-uh-*nye*-us
ANTIOCH   *An*-tee-ock
ANTIOCHUS EPIPHANES
   An-*tie*-uh-kus ee-*pih*-fah-neez
ANTONIA   An-*toe*-nee-uh
AQUILA   Uh-*kwil*-uh
ARABIA   Uh-*ray*-bee-uh
ARTAXERXES   Are-tuh-*zerk*-seez
ASIA MINOR   *Aye*-zha *my*-ner
ASSYRIA   Uh-*sear*-ee-uh
BAAL   *Bay*-ul or *Bah*-al
BABEL   *Bay*-buhl
BABYLONIA   Bab-uh-*lo*-nee-uh
BARNABAS   *Bar*-nuh-bus
BARTHOLOMEW   Bar-*thol*-o-mew
BELSHAZZAR   Bel-*shazz*-er
BENJAMIN   *Ben*-juh-mun
BETHABARA   Beth-*ab*-uh-ruh
BETHANY   *Beth*-uh-nee
BETHLEHEM   *Beth*-luh-hem
BETHSAIDA   Beth-*say*-uh-duh
BUL   Bool
CAESAREA   Sess-uh-*ree*-uh or
   See-zur-ree-uh
CAIN   Kayn
CALEB   *Kay*-leb
CANAAN   *Kay*-nun
CANAANITE   *Kay*-nan-ite
CAPERNAUM   Kuh-*per*-nay-um
CEPHAS   *See*-fus
CHALDEANS   Kal-*dee*-unz
CHISLEAU   Kis-*lay*
CHRONICLES   *Kron*-ih-kuls
COLOSSIANS   Kuh-*losh*-unz
CORINTH   *Kor*-inth
CORINTHIANS   Koe-*rin*-thee-unz

CORNELIUS   Kor-*nee*-lih-us or
   Kor-*neel*-yus
CYPRUS   *Sye*-prus
CYRUS   *Sye*-rus
DAMASCUS   Duh-*mas*-kus
DECAPOLIS   Dee-*kap*-uh-lis
DERBE   *Der*-bee
DEUTERONOMY   Due-ter-*ahn*-o-mee
ECCLESIASTES   Ee-*klee*-zee-*as*-tez
EDOM   *Ee*-dum
EGYPT   *Ee*-jipt
ELEAZAR   El-e-*a*-zar or Ee-li-*a*-zar
ELI   *Ee*-lye
ELIJAH   Ee-*lye*-juh
ELISHA   Ee-*lye*-shuh
ELUL   Eh-*lool*
EMMAUS   Em-*may*-us
EPHESIANS   E-*fee*-shunz
EPHESUS   *Ef*-uh-sus
ESTHER   *Es*-ter
ETHANIM   Aye-thuh-*neem*
ETHIOPIAN   Ee-thee-*o*-pee-un
EUPHRATES   You-*fray*-teez
EXODUS   *Ex*-o-dus
EZEKIEL   Ee-*zeek*-yul or
   Ee-*zeek*-ee-ul
EZRA   *Ez*-ruh
GALATIANS   Guh-*lay*-shunz
GALILEE   *Gal*-uh-lee
GAMALIEL   Guh-*may*-lih-ul
GENESIS   *Jen*-uh-sus
GIDEON   *Gid*-e-un
GOLIATH   Go-*lye*-uth
HABAKKUK   Huh-*bak*-kuk
HAGGAI   *Hag*-gye
HANNAH   *Han*-uh
HANNUKKAH   *Hah*-nuk-kuh
HARAN   *Ha*-run
HELLENIZATION   *Hel*-uh-nuh-*zay*-shun
HELLESPONT   *Hel*-uh-spont
HEROD   *Hair*-ud
HEZEKIAH   Hez-uh-*kye*-uh
HOSEA   Ho-*zay*-uh
HULDAH   *Hul*-duh
ICONIUM   Eye-*ko*-nee-um
ISAAC   *Eye*-zuk
ISAIAH   Eye-*zay*-uh
ISRAEL   *Iz*-ray-el
JACOB   *Jay*-kub
JAIRUS   *Jeye*-rus

8

JAPHETH *Jay*-futh
JEHOIAKIM Jeh-*hoy*-uh-kim
JEREMIAH Jair-uh-*my*-uh
JEROBOAM Jair-uh-*bo*-um
JETHRO *Jeth*-row
JEZEBEL *Jez*-uh-bel
JOB Job (o as in Ohio)
JONAH *Jo*-nuh
JONATHAN *John*-uh-thun
JORDAN *Jor*-dun
JOSEPH *Jo*-sef
JOSHUA *Josh*-yew-uh
JUDAH *Joo*-duh
JUDAS *Joo*-dus
JUDEA Joo-*dee*-uh
LAMENTATIONS Lam-en-*tay*-shunz
LEVI *Lee*-vye
LEVITICUS Lih-*vit*-ih-kus
LYDIA *Lid*-e-uh
LYSTRA *Liss*-truh
MACCABEUS Mack-uh-*bee*-us
MACEDONIA Mass-uh-*doe*-nee-uh
MALACHI *Mal*-uh-kye
MALTA *Mahl*-tuh
MANASSEH Muh-*nass*-uh
MATTHIAS Muh-*thie*-us
MELITA *Mel*-i-tuh
MESOPOTAMIA *Mes*-uh-puh-*tay*-me-uh
MICAH *My*-kuh
MILETUS My-*lee*-tus
MOSES *Mo*-zez
MOUNT ARARAT Mownt *Air*-rat
MOUNT SINAI Mownt *Sy*-nye
NAHUM *Nay*-hum
NATHAN *Nay*-thun
NATHANAEL Nuh-*than*-a-el or
  Nuh-*than*-yel
NAZARETH *Naz*-uh-reth
NEBUCHADNEZZAR *Neb*-uh-kud-*nez*-zer
NEHEMIAH Nee-huh-*my*-uh
NERO *Nee*-row
NICODEMUS Nick-uh-*dee*-mus
NILE Nyl
NINEVEH *Nin*-uh-vuh
NISAN *Nee*-san
NOAH *No*-uh
OBADIAH O-buh-*die*-uh
PALESTINE *Pal*-uh-styn
PATMOS *Pat*-muss
PEREA Peh-*ree*-uh
PERSIAN GULF *Per*-zhuhn guhlf
PHARAOH *Fay*-row
PHILEMON Fie-*lee*-mum or
  Fih-*lee*-mun
PHILIP *Fil*-uhp
PHILIPPI *Fil*-uh-pie or Fuh-*lip*-pie

PHILIPPIANS Ful-*lip*-pee-unz
PHOENICIA Fih-*nish*-uh
POMPEY *Pahm*-pee
PRISCILLA Pri-*sil*-uh
PROVERBS *Prah*-verbz
PSALMS Salmz
PTOLEMY *Tol*-uh-me
PURIM *Pew*-rim
PUTEOLI Pew-*tee*-o-li
RAHAB *Ray*-hab
REHOBOAM Re-ho-*bo*-um
REUBEN *Rew*-ben
REVELATION Rev-uh-*la*-shun
ROSH HASHANAH
  Rahsh Hah-*shah*-nah
SAMARIA Suh-*meh*-ree-uh
SAMSON *Sam*-sun
SAPPHIRA Suh-*fye*-ruh
SEBAT Shuh-*vaht*
SELEUCUS Seh-*loo*-kuss
SENNACHERIB Sen-*nak*-er-ib
SERGIUS PAULUS *Sir*-ji-us *Pawl*-us
SHEBA *Shee*-buh
SHEM Sheem
SIDON *Sye*-dun
SIMEON *Sim*-ee-un
SIMON *Sye*-mun
SIVAN See-*vahn*
SOLOMON *Sol*-o-mun
STEPHEN *Ste*-ven
SYRIA *Sear*-ee-uh
SYROPHOENICIA *Sye*-row-fih-*nish*-uh
TABITHA *Tab*-ih-thuh
TARSUS *Tar*-sus
TEBETH Tay-*vayth* or Tay-*vayt*
TETRARCHY *Teh*-trar-kee
THADDEUS *Tha*-dee-us
THAMMOZ Tah-*mooz*
THESSALONIANS *Thes*-uh-*low*-nee-unz
THESSALONICA *Thes*-uh-luh-*nye*-kuh
TIGRIS *Tye*-griss
TIMOTHY *Tim*-o-thee
TITUS *Tye*-tuss
TIZRI Tish-*ree*
TROAS *Tro*-az
TYRE Tire
UR Er
ZACCHEUS Zack-*kee*-us
ZACHARIAS Zack-uh-*rye*-us
ZEALOT *Zel*-ut
ZEBEDEE *Zeb*-eh-dee
ZECHARIAH Zek-uh-*rye*-uh
ZEDEKIAH Zed-uh-*kye*-uh
ZEPHANIAH Zef-uh-*nye*-uh
ZERUBBABEL Zuh-*ru*-buh-bul
ZIF Ziv

9

How We Got Our Bible

Lesson 1

ORIGIN OF THE BIBLE

A. Divine Source

The Bible came from God. Other books present the evidence of this; here we merely note that such a book never has come and never would come from man alone.

B. Human Writers

1. God used about forty men in writing the Bible. Some of these writers are unknown, such as the writers of the last chapter of Deuteronomy, the book of Job, and some of the psalms. In round numbers, the time in which the forty worked included about fifteen hundred years, from 1400 B.C. to A.D. 100.

2. The perfect harmony of these writings is convincing evidence that all of them were guided by a single mind—the mind of God. Some of the writers simply wrote down what God had told them, as when Moses wrote the law (Deuteronomy 31:24). Some of them wrote what they had seen, as when Matthew recorded what Jesus had done in his presence. Some of them no doubt recorded what they had learned from others, as when Luke wrote about the birth of Jesus, probably repeating what Mary had told him. Some of them may have used earlier writings, as when the writer of 2 Samuel 1:18 referred to the book of Jasher, a book that had been lost. But all the writers were specially guided by the Spirit of God so that they wrote just what God wanted them to write. Men so guided by God's Spirit are called *inspired* men. Such men wrote God's Word for us.

C. Purpose of This Lesson

Much might be written about how men were inspired, but this lesson is rather a study of how the Bible has been *transmitted* to us after it was written by the original authors. We do not have a single book in the handwriting of Moses or Isaiah or Paul. How do we know the Bible we have is the Word as written by the original writers?

1. God did not inspire all who copied or translated the Bible, as He did the original writers, so that they could not make mistakes. It is evident that both copyists and translators could and did make errors.

2. But many ancient manuscripts and translations have been preserved. By comparing them, we can usually find the mistakes that have been made. In a few cases we cannot be sure exactly what the original writing was, but none of these cases have any effect on our Christian faith or life.

ANCIENT VERSIONS AND MANUSCRIPTS

While we have no part of the Bible in the handwriting of the original author himself, we have two kinds of sources from which we can learn what the original writers wrote. These are manuscripts and versions.

A. Definitions

1. *Manuscripts* are documents written by hand. Before printing was invented, this was the only way of producing books. We have no Bible manuscripts written by the original authors, but we

11

have many copies: that is, manuscripts copied from the original manuscripts or from copies of them. In this lesson we use the word manuscripts to mean copies written by hand in the same language used by the original writers.

2. A _version_ is a translation of any document into another language. Some ancient versions were translated from manuscripts older than any we now have. Therefore they help us to know just what the original writer wrote.

B. Old Testament Scriptures

1. _Manuscripts_. The Old Testament books were written in the Hebrew language between 1400 B.C. and 400 B.C. The oldest Bible manuscripts now known are the Scripture portions among the Dead Sea scrolls, which were found in caves near the Dead Sea in 1947 and the years following. Probably it was about 100 B.C. when these manuscripts were copied from earlier copies.

There are many Old Testament manuscripts that were copied in later centuries.

2. _Versions_. The oldest version of the Old Testament is a Greek version called the _Septuagint_ (pronounced _Sep_-tu-a-jint). From the Latin word for seventy, this name was given because the translation was made by about seventy Jewish scholars in Alexandria, Egypt. Being made about 250 B.C. from Hebrew manuscripts older than any we have now, this version helps us to know what the original writers wrote.

Other important Greek versions include those of Theodotion, Aquila, and Symmachus, which were translated in the second century after Christ. There were also ancient versions in Syriac, Egyptian, Ethiopic, Armenian, and other languages.

C. New Testament Scriptures

1. _Manuscripts_. All the books of the New Testament were written in Greek during the first century after Christ. The oldest New Testament manuscripts now known were copied about three hundred years later, around A.D. 350. Only two known manuscripts are of this age. They are called the _Sinaitic_ and _Vatican_ man-

uscripts (prounounced Sy-nay-_it_-ik and _Vat_-i-can).

The _Sinaitic_ Manuscript is so called because it was discovered in 1844 in a monastery at the foot of Mount Sinai. It is now in the British Museum.

The _Vatican_ Manuscript was placed in the library of the Vatican soon after that library was established in 1448, and is still kept there.

The _Alexandrian_ Manuscript, copied about A.D. 400 or a little later, is in the British Museum. In 1628 it was a gift to King Charles I from the patriarch of Constantinople, who had brought it from Alexandria, Egypt, at an earlier time.

There are more than a hundred other manuscripts dating from the fifth to the tenth century and called _uncial_ manuscripts. Derived from the Latin word for inch, this term indicates that these manuscripts were written in letters an inch high. Actually this is an exaggeration, but writers of those centuries used large capital letters only. In the ninth and tenth centuries a new style of writing was developed, using small letters. This kind of writing is called _cursive_ or running. There are hundreds of cursive manuscripts dating between the ninth century and the invention of printing in the fifteenth century.

2. _Versions_. Perhaps in the first half of the second century the Bible was translated into the Syriac, and not much later into the Latin. A more careful Latin version was completed about 400. Called the Vulgate, which means common or popular, this version became the official Bible of the Roman Catholic Church and of western Europe. Probably in the third and fourth centuries versions were made also in Coptic (Egyptian), Gothic, Ethiopic, and Armenian. Made from very ancient manuscripts, all of these help us to be sure the Bible we have is approximately the same as the original writings.

ENGLISH VERSIONS

A. Old English Versions

There were people in the British Isles in the early days of the church, but the English people and the English language developed later. There was an early need for God's Word in the native tongue.

1. In 735 the Venerable Bede, then at the point of death, finished his translation of John's Gospel into Anglo-Saxon, one of the languages from which English developed.

2. About 900, King Alfred translated portions of the Bible. Later came the Norman conquest led by William the Conqueror, and in the course of time the Norman French language blended with the Anglo-Saxon to become what is sometimes called Middle English.

3. About 1380 Wycliffe and his co-workers translated the Bible into Middle English. These early translations were not made from the Greek and Hebrew, but from the Latin Vulgate, which was the official Bible of the church in that time.

4. In 1525 William Tyndale brought out an English version of the New Testament. In the following years he added translations of Old Testament books. Tyndale translated directly from the original Greek and Hebrew instead of translating the Latin translation into English, but no doubt he did compare the familiar Latin version and obtain help from it. The printing press had now been invented, so it was possible to produce thousands of copies at small expense. In a short time, the Scriptures were distributed more widely than ever before.

5. English churchmen angrily opposed the work of Tyndale, but the popular demand was so strong that both the churchmen and the king (Henry VIII) approved the translation made by Myles Coverdale in 1535. Not knowing Hebrew and Greek, Coverdale used the Latin Vulgate and Luther's German translation. But he undoubtedly was influenced also by Tyndale's version, which had been made from the original languages. Other translations followed, all strongly influenced by Tyndale.

6. Opposition to the English Bible again arose when Mary Tudor came to the throne and exerted strong efforts to bring England again under the power of the Roman church. Some of the best English scholars fled to Europe. In Geneva, William Whittington and others produced a revised English Bible, based largely on earlier English versions. Completing this "Geneva Bible" in 1560, they dedicated it to England's new queen, Elizabeth.

7. Some of the marginal notes in the Geneva Bible offended the bishops of the Church of England, and they responded by producing a new version of their own. This "Bishops' Bible" was published in 1568.

8. Through the rest of that century, the clergymen used the Bishops' Bible in the churches; but the Geneva Bible was preferred by many of the people, especially the Puritans who were intent on reforming some practices of the church. In 1604, King James appointed a committee of fifty-four scholars to prepare a new version. They followed the Bishops' Bible except where they thought changes were needed; but they used other English translations, the German, the Greek and Hebrew texts, the Syriac, the Septuagint, and several Latin versions. The result of their labors was the King James Version, published in 1611 and still the most used Bible in the English language.

B. Revised English Versions

Any living language is constantly changing. Many words used in the King James Version are now almost unknown. Examples are "neesings," "besom," "wist." Other words have changed their meanings. For example, "let" formerly meant to hinder (Romans 1:13), but now it means to permit. Another word that has changed its meaning is "conversation." To us today it means talk, but to the English people of King James' day it meant the whole way of living. Unless we recognize that old meaning, we miss the point of such passages as 2 Peter 2:7 and 3:11.

1. In the course of centuries, therefore, scholars began to see a need to revise the King James Version. In 1885 a *Revised Version* was produced by a committee of fifty-one British scholars, assisted by thirty-two Americans.

2. In 1901 the American members of the committee brought out the *American Standard Version*, introducing some

variations more in accord with American usage of English. This *American Standard Version* has been hailed as the most accurate translation in the English language.

C. Modern English Versions

While they dropped many obsolete words, the revised versions named above kept old pronouns such as "thou" and verb forms such as "doest." This allowed a more exact translation. In the American Standard Version, for example, "thou" and "thee" are always singular, while "ye" and "you" are always plural. Thus they accurately reflect the distinctions found in the original languages; but in modern English "you" is used for both singular and plural. Also, *thou* and *ye* are always in the nominative case, while *thee* and *you* are always in the objective. But in modern English, *you* is both nominative and objective, so the distinctions of the Greek and Hebrew are lost. Nevertheless there are many who think the Scriptures should be available in the kind of English that is commonly used.

1. A number of modern translations have been produced, each the work of one man.

2. The *Revised Standard Version,* completed in 1952, is the work of a committee of American scholars.

3. *The New English Bible,* prepared by a British committee, was completed in 1961.

4. The *New American Standard Version* was published in 1963.

5. The *New International Version* was completed in 1978.

6. *The New King James Version* was introduced in 1982.

QUESTIONS

1. Who is the ultimate source of the Bible?

_____

2. About how many human writers of the Bible were there?

_____

3. Through how many years was the writing done?

_____

4. How can we account for the perfect harmony of all these writings?

_____

5. Since we have no Bible books in the handwriting of their authors, what two kinds of documents help us to know what was in the books as they were originally written?

_____

6. In what language was the Old Testament originally written?

_____

7. In what language was the New Testament originally written?

_____

8. The oldest known Bible manuscripts are among the Dead Sea Scrolls. About when were they made?

_____

9. What version became the official Bible of the Roman Catholic church?

_____

10. When was the King James Version published?

_____

11. Name some English versions newer than the King James.

_____

_____

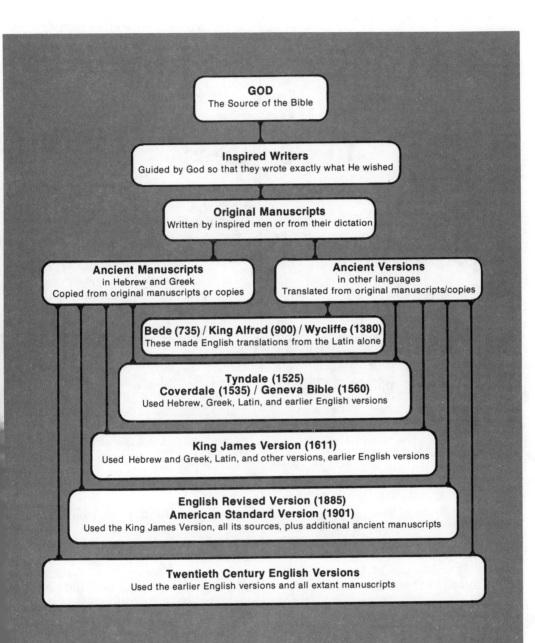

GOD
The Source of the Bible

Inspired Writers
Guided by God so that they wrote exactly what He wished

Original Manuscripts
Written by inspired men or from their dictation

Ancient Manuscripts
in Hebrew and Greek
Copied from original manuscripts or copies

Ancient Versions
in other languages
Translated from original manuscripts/copies

Bede (735) / King Alfred (900) / Wycliffe (1380)
These made English translations from the Latin alone

Tyndale (1525)
Coverdale (1535) / Geneva Bible (1560)
Used Hebrew, Greek, Latin, and earlier English versions

King James Version (1611)
Used Hebrew and Greek, Latin, and other versions, earlier English versions

English Revised Version (1885)
American Standard Version (1901)
Used the King James Version, all its sources, plus additional ancient manuscripts

Twentieth Century English Versions
Used the earlier English versions and all extant manuscripts

God's Word to Us

GOD'S WORD

The Bible is God's Word. Other books have been written to prove this, but in this book we take it as already proved. Let us think of what this means.

A. God speaks with authority.

1. *Authority is needed.* Without it a baseball game would become a riot, an army would become a mob, a nation could not exist, religion would be no more than imagination or "wishful thinking." Baseball finds the needed authority in its rule book, the army in its orders, a nation in its constitution, religion in its Bible.

2. *Inadequate sources of authority* have been suggested and accepted by some.

    a. Writings of thinkers such as Confucius, Buddha, Mohammed, Plato.

    b. Writings of literary men such as Milton, Shakespeare, Longfellow.

    c. Pronouncements of church officials such as bishops, cardinals, popes.

    d. The findings of scientists such as Newton, Darwin, Einstein.

    e. One's own mind or conscience or experience.

3. *God is the supreme authority* because He created all things, He knows all things, and He is able to control all things. The Bible carries authority because it is His Word. It is His way of making His will known to us.

4. *Man's welfare depends on his acceptance of proper authority.* One who defies the laws of his state or nation is a criminal or a rebel. He may be imprisoned or put to death. What fate can one expect if he defies the Word of Almighty God?

B. The Bible as God's Word

1. *The Bible is a special revelation from God.* It was written by inspired men, men specially guided by God's Spirit so that they wrote just what God wanted them to write. Through the Bible God tells us things that we could never learn in any other way. Some of them are mentioned here. Can you think of others?

    a. The nature of God. See Genesis 17:1; Exodus 34:6, 7; John 3:16.

    b. The duty of man. See Ecclesiastes 12:13; Micah 6:8; Matthew 5:1—7:29.

    c. The origin of earthly things. See Genesis 1:1—2:25; Psalm 104:1-24; John 1:1-3.

    d. The destiny of men and the world. See Mark 16:15, 16; Matthew 25:31-46; 2 Peter 3:10-14; Revelation 21:1—22:7.

2. *The purpose of Bible study.* Many purposes may be suggested, but here we mention two of the most important. Add as many others as you wish.

    a. To know God. If we come to know the Book but do not come to know God, we have failed and the purpose of God has been defeated.

    b. To guide our lives. If we come to know the Book but do not come to live by the Book, this too is failure. Read James 1:22.

3. *Our attitude toward the Bible.* God's Word is holy. It deserves not only

our study, but our reverent study. Its treasures are missed by one who approaches it with a skeptical or faultfinding attitude. One who reads it as a message from God is richly rewarded.

TO US

God has given His Word, but it has no effect in our lives unless it actually comes *to us:* unless we receive it and study it and understand it and obey it. As we try to understand the Bible, several rules are helpful. Study those given below and keep them in mind whenever you study the Bible in the future.

A. Each Scripture is to be understood in the light of all other Scriptures.

An example may be seen in the answers given to people seeking salvation. One was told to believe in Jesus. (Acts 16:30, 31), others were told to repent and be baptized (Acts 2:37, 38), and another was told to be baptized and wash away his sins (Acts 22:16). But when we study further, we see that there is no contradiction or confusion here. Each one was told what he should do *at that particular time.* When we know the whole story, it is plain that all the converts believed, and repented, and were baptized.

B. A distinction is to be made between the Old Testament and the New Testament.

1. The Old Testament foretold a new and different covenant (Jeremiah 31:31-34); the book of Hebrews explains at length that this new and better covenant has replaced the old one. We are under the new covenant, not the law of the Old Testament.

2. Early in the history of the church an effort was made to bring all Christians under the Old Testament law, but Christian leaders, guided by the Holy Spirit, rejected that attempt (Acts 15:1-29). We can safely follow their example and reject a similar attempt whenever it is made.

3. Nevertheless it is profitable to study the Old Testament as well as the New (2 Timothy 3:16, 17; 1 Corinthians 10:11). The Old helps us understand the New (Galatians 3:24, 25); it tells much about our Saviour (Isaiah 53); it helps us to know God (Exodus 34:6, 7); it helps to guide our living (Micah 6:8).

C. Any passage of Scripture is to be studied in its immediate context. Such questions as the following should be considered. When these are answered correctly, we are less likely to misunderstand the message of God's Word.

1. *Who is speaking?* The whole Bible is God's Word, but sometimes God's Word quotes the word of someone else. For example, Genesis 3:4, 5 quotes a lie told by a serpent that doubtless was inspired by Satan. This lie was in direct contradiction with God's statement quoted in Genesis 2:17. Mark 9:5 quotes a mistaken suggestion of Simon Peter. This suggestion should not be attributed to God; in fact, God promptly corrected it (Mark 9:7, 8). We should not think a lie of Satan or a mistake of man is God's truth just because it is recorded truthfully in God's Word.

2. *To whom is he speaking?* The angel's announcement in Luke 1:26-33 was spoken to Mary, but the teaching of Romans 12 was given to all the Christians in Rome. Ephesians 5:22—6:9 has messages directed especially to wives, husbands, children, fathers, servants, and masters.

3. *Is the passage intended for others in addition to those to whom it was first given?* It is generally agreed that the announcement to Mary cannot be applied to anyone else, but the instructions in Romans 12 are for all Christians everywhere. The messages from Ephesians that were mentioned above are no doubt intended for all Christian families, employees, and employers.

4. *Is the passage intended to apply to a limited time or under specific circumstances, or is it of universal application?* Paul once wrote to Timothy, "Use a little wine for thy stomach's sake and thine often infirmities" (1 Timothy 5:23). Doubtless this was excellent advice under the circumstances, but it can hardly be applied to anyone else unless he has the same stomach trouble Timothy had—and even then it may be that a better medicine is available under present circumstances.

QUESTIONS

1. Mention some inadequate sources of authority.

_____

_____

_____

_____

2. Why is God's authority supreme?

_____

_____

3. Mention some things that are revealed to us by the Bible.

_____

_____

_____

4. Give some purposes of Bible study.

_____

_____

5. What is the proper attitude toward the Bible? Why?

_____

_____

6. Give some simple rules for Bible study.

_____

_____

_____

_____

_____

7. Give an example of how one Scripture may help us understand another.

_____

_____

_____

8. Tell something about the distinction between the Old Testament and the New.

_____

_____

_____

9. Why is it sometimes important to know who is speaking in a particular passage of Scripture?

_____

_____

_____

_____

10. Why is it important to know for whom a passage is intended?

_____

_____

11. Give an example of a passage intended to apply under specific circumstances.

_____

_____

_____

Divisions of the Bible

Lesson 3

Though usually bound in a single volume, the Bible is really a collection of sixty-six books. The importance of this can be seen by comparing this collection with a home library.

Suppose I have a thousand books on history, poetry, science, mathematics, geography, and theology. They have information on practically every subject.

Then suppose I want to know something about Henry VIII of England, so I reach for the nearest book. If it is a book of Riley's poems, I may read it all without finding what I want. I should have selected a book of English history.

Now suppose I want to know what to do to be saved. I am sure the information is in the Bible. So I merely open the Bible and start to read. If I happen to be reading the book of Joshua, I can read a long time and fail to find the information I want, because I am reading Old Testament history, a record of the times before salvation in Christ was offered. What I need is Acts, a history of the time when Christ's apostles were explaining the way of salvation.

TWO LARGE DIVISIONS

The two largest divisions of the Bible

are the Old Testament and the New Testament.

DIVISIONS OF THE OLD TESTAMENT

The books of the Old Testament fall naturally into four groups, which are easily memorized: Law, History, Poetry, and Prophecy.

A. Exceptions to the Classification

The names given to the four divisions give a general idea of what is in them, but no division is limited to one kind of literature. For example, the books of law contain also history, poetry, and prophecy; the books of history and poetry have prophecy too; and the books of prophecy have much history and poetry.

B. The Message of Each Division

1. *The books of law* are the first five books of the Bible. They trace God's dealing with mankind from "the beginning" through the flood of Noah's time, through the beginning of the Hebrew nation in Abraham, Isaac, and Jacob, through their escape from Egypt and their wandering in the wilderness, to the time when Moses died and his people were ready to enter the Promised Land with Joshua as their leader.

All this history provides the setting in which God gave the Hebrew people the law that fills a large part of this group of books. This is sometimes called the Jewish law or the Old Testament law. The best-known parts of it are the Ten Commandments (Exodus 20:3-17), the greatest of all commandments (Deuteronomy 6:5), and the commandment second in importance (Leviticus 19:18).

It is notable that Moses still stands as the greatest of lawgivers, greater than Hammurabi, Solon, or any other. The divine law he delivered is reflected even now in the laws of civilized peoples, including our own.

This whole group of books reveals God as the great Creator. More than that, it reveals Him as an interested, loving, patient Father ever striving to bless man, whom He created in His own image.

2. *The books of history* begin with Joshua and end with Esther. They record much of the preparation for the coming of Christ, and their influence in the world is greater than that of any other history except that recorded in the New Testament.

These books of history cover a period of about a thousand years, from the conquest of the Promised Land about 1400 B.C. to the end of the Old Testament about 400 B.C. Naturally, they cannot tell everything that happened, but they record the course of history in a general way and show clearly the effects of following God's law and of ignoring it. The books deal principally with the Hebrews because it was through them that the Christ was to come.

3. *The books of poetry* have a large influence on the sacred music and worship even of the present day. Psalms are sung in many languages by millions of Christians and Jews. The lyric poetry of the Hebrews was at its height nearly a thousand years before the lyrics of Horace. The writer of Ecclesiastes discussed the world's vanity five hundred years before Socrates talked in Athens. Some of the psalms are nearly a thousand years older than Ovid, yet today these ancient songs are sung by more people than ever before. Other ancient poetry is known to only a few scholars, but the poetry of the Bible is held and honored in millions of devout hearts. How shall we account for these facts unless we agree that Bible poetry is inspired of God?

4. *The prophetic books* include some of the finest literature ever written in any language. The student of the Bible, however, is not chiefly interested in literary value. His question is this: Are these books really messages from God; and if so, what is God saying to us in them? This cannot be answered fully in a paragraph; but these books do bring one convincing proof of the inspiration of both the Old Testament and the New Testament and of the divinity of Christ. Lesson 17 lists some of the prophecies that were fulfilled in Christ.

DIVISIONS OF THE NEW TESTAMENT

Just as there are four kinds of books in the Old Testament, so there are four kinds in the New Testament: Gospels, History, Letters, Prophecy.

A. Purposes of the Four Groups

In studying any passage of Scripture, it is important to know to whom it is addressed. In this we are helped by knowing in a general way the purpose of each kind of book.

For example, Acts is a book of history, recording the beginning of the church and telling how people became Christians. "Repent, and be baptized" (Acts 2:38) is not addressed to Christians, but to non-Christians.

On the other hand, the letters are written to Christians to help them live as Christ would have them live. In one of them we read, "Pure religion and undefiled before God and the Father is this, To visit the fatherless and widows in their affliction, and to keep himself unspotted from the world" (James 1:27). This is addressed to Christians, not to non-Christians.

A non-Christian should not ignore Acts 2:38, which is addressed to him, and try to follow James 1:27, which is not addressed to him. And a Christian should not be content because he has obeyed Acts 2:38, which was addressed to him in his former condition. He should now follow James 1:27, which is addressed to him in his present condition as a Christian.

1. *The Gospels* tell about the life, death, and resurrection of Jesus. Their purpose is to lead us to believe that He is the Christ, the Son of God. John 20:31 states this purpose.

2. *The book of history*, Acts, tells how the church began and carried on its work, and how people became Christians. Its purpose is to show people today how to become Christians and carry on the work of the church.

3. *The letters* are addressed to Christians. Their purpose is to guide Christians in their living, helping them to do whatever Jesus commanded. See Matthew 28:20. Romans 12 is a good example of their teaching.

4. *The book of prophecy*, Revelation, tells of the final victory of Christ and His people. Its purpose is to encourage us to keep on living as Christians ought to live. Its message is summed up as follows:

"Be thou faithful unto death, and I will give thee a crown of life" (Revelation 2:10).

B. Some Facts About the Four Groups

1. *The Gospels* record a time of transition. They are properly listed as a part of the New Testament, but in the period they cover the Old Testament law was still in effect. Jesus lived in the Jewish, or Mosaic, dispensation. He was circumcised according to the law; He worshiped in the synagogues; when one asked Him what good thing to do to inherit eternal life, He referred to the Old Testament law. Nevertheless He was preparing for the time of the new covenant, and training His apostles to be its messengers. The new dispensation was dramatically ushered in on the Day of Pentecost, fifty days after Jesus rose from the dead.

While Jesus walked among men, He and John the Baptist and the apostles preached the gospel of the kingdom, saying, "The kingdom of God is at hand." They could not yet preach the gospel that Peter and Paul and the other apostles preached later: "That Christ died for our sins according to the scriptures . . . and that he rose again the third day according to the scriptures" (1 Corinthians 15:3, 4). But Jesus was preparing His apostles to preach that gospel when the proper time came.

During the period of the Gospels, Jesus was here in the flesh, walking among men as Lord and Master. He could and did say to one, "Thy sins are forgiven thee," to another, "Thy faith hath made thee whole," to another, "Rise, take up thy bed, and walk," and to a thief on a cross, "Today shalt thou be with me in paradise." But when His work of preparation was completed by His death and resurrection, He sent the Holy Spirit to guide His chosen apostles as they proclaimed the way of salvation for all men in all climes and in all times. That way is taught in the whole New Testament.

2. *The book of history* in the New Testament is the book of Acts. It tells how the church began and grew as the

apostles obeyed the great commission of Matthew 28:19, 20. Since the Holy Spirit guided these men, we know we are following the leading of the Holy Spirit when we teach as they taught and bring men to Christ in the same way they did.

3. *The letters* tell Christians how they ought to live, how to do what Jesus taught. However, not all their teaching is intended for all Christians. There are instructions for new Christians or "babes" in Christ, and there are instructions for those who have lived in Christ and should have gone far in Christian attainment. There are instructions for deacons and elders. There are instructions for widows, for parents, for children. There are instructions for servants and masters. But of course there are many parts of the letters that do give instructions for all who are trying to follow Christ. Romans 12 is an example.

4. *The book of prophecy,* Revelation, is perhaps less read and less understood than any other New Testament book. Two things make it difficult to understand this book. First, some of the language is highly figurative and symbolic, and we cannot be sure of the meaning of some of the symbols. Second, prophecies of the distant future are often hard to understand. In Jesus' time the Old Testament prophecies concerning Him were understood so poorly that many of the trained scholars opposed Him and demanded that He be put to death. So it is likely that scholars of the Christian era will fail to understand the prophecies of Revelation until those prophecies have been fulfilled.

However, the book as a whole brings a helpful and encouraging message that every Christian reader can easily grasp. It is obviously a book on faithfulness, calling us to be true to Christ regardless of all difficulties, and promising the final victory of righteousness.

QUESTIONS

1. Give the divisions of the Old Testament and the number of books in each.

_____

_____

2. What is there besides law in the books of law?

_____

3. How long a time is covered by the books of history?

_____

4. Though they are thousands of years old, the psalms are the best-known and best-loved poems in the world. How do you account for this?

_____

_____

5. How could Old Testament prophets foretell events that occurred centuries later?

_____

6. Give the divisions of the New Testament and the number of books in each.

_____

_____

_____

_____

7. Briefly tell the purpose of the Gospels.

_____

8. What purpose is seen in Acts?

_____

_____

9. What is the purpose of the letters?

_____

10. What is the purpose of Revelation?

_____

Books of the Old Testament

Lesson 4

A carpenter should know his tool chest. He must know a saw from a square, know the purpose of each and how to use each. Also he should know where in the chest to find the tool he needs for any particular job.

The Bible is the Christian's tool chest. In Christian teaching and in winning people to Christ, no human reasoning can equal the Scriptures themselves. There is a Scripture to fit every need, and the Christian should know where to find the one he needs at a particular time. A start in this direction is to learn to name the books of the Bible in order. It is easy to learn the Old Testament books in one evening.

BOOKS OF LAW

There are five books of law: Genesis, Exodus, Leviticus, Numbers, Deuteronomy. Memorize the names of them now.

These five books are called the Pentateuch (pronounced *pen*-ta-teuk), from the Greek *penta,* five, and *teuchos,* book. According to an ancient tradition never disproved, they were written mostly by Moses. The last chapter, telling of Moses' death, probably was added by another writer, possibly Joshua.

1. *Genesis* means *beginning.* The book of Genesis is the only dependable record of the beginning of the world. Moses needed divine guidance in order to tell of the events of creation, because they occurred when no man was there to observe and record them. God revealed to Moses what had happened.

Genesis also traces briefly the history of mankind through many centuries until the children of Israel were living in Egypt about 1500 B.C.

2. *Exodus* means *going out.* This book tells how the people of Israel went out of Egypt and at Mount Sinai received from God the law that was to govern them as an independent nation under God.

3. *Leviticus* takes its name from the tribe of Levi, one of the twelve tribes of Israel. All the men of this tribe were dedicated to religious service. One family of them became priests, and the rest were assistants to the priests, musicians in the choir and orchestra, caretakers in the tabernacle or temple, and so on. The book of Leviticus contains special laws for the Levites and worship.

4. *Numbers* is so called because it tells how the people of Israel were twice numbered, or counted, in national censuses. It also records parts of the law not included in Exodus, and tells of the wandering of Israel in the desert between Sinai and the Promised Land.

5. *Deuteronomy* means the second law or *repeated law*. It records Moses' final addresses to his people, in which he repeated much of the law recorded in Exodus.

BOOKS OF HISTORY

The books of history are twelve—too many to be counted on the fingers. They can be memorized very easily, however, if they are listed in three groups of three, with the central group having three pairs instead of three single books. Learn them by saying them aloud or by writing them as follows:

Joshua	1 Samuel	Ezra
Judges	2 Samuel	Nehemiah
Ruth	1 Kings	Esther
	2 Kings	
	1 Chronicles	
	2 Chronicles	

These books cover about a thousand years, from 1400 B.C. to 400 B.C.

1. The three books in the first column tell how Israel conquered the Promised Land and lived there with the judges as their leaders.

2. The three pairs of books in the center column tell how Israel became a monarchy and rose to be one of the great nations of the world, how that nation was divided and weakened, and how its people finally were made captives by the Assyrians and Babylonians.

3. The three books in the right column tell of events in Palestine and in Persia after the Babylonian captivity was ended.

BOOKS OF POETRY

There are five books of poetry: Job, Psalms, Proverbs, Ecclesiastes, and Song of Solomon. Memorize these names, using the fingers of your hand if they will help. From the standpoint of age, influence, permanence, and beauty,

these books are seen to tower above all the other poetry of the world.

1. *Job* is a dramatic debate in poetic form, dealing with the problem of human suffering. It brings a lesson of unfaltering trust in God.

2. *Psalms* is a collection of songs, many of them by David. No doubt many of them were specially written for use in the worship services.

3. *Proverbs* is a collection of short, pointed sayings. Most of them were written by Solomon.

4. *Ecclesiastes* means the *preacher*. This is the name given to himself by Solomon, who wrote the book (Ecclesiastes 1:1). His sermon deals with the uselessness of much human activity. Its conclusion is stated in Ecclesiastes 12:13.

5. The *Song of Solomon* is an operetta, probably the work of Solomon. The action cannot be traced with certainty because there are no stage directions, but we do understand that this is a beautiful and moving love story. Many regard it as a prophecy of the love between Christ and His church.

BOOKS OF PROPHECY

There are seventeen books of prophecy. For easy memorizing they can be listed in four groups, with five in the first group and four in each of the others. Take time to learn them thoroughly and review them often.

MAJOR PROPHETS
Isaiah
Jeremiah
Lamentations
Ezekiel
Daniel

MINOR PROPHETS

Hosea	Jonah	Zephaniah
Joel	Micah	Haggai
Amos	Nahum	Zechariah
Obadiah	Habakkuk	Malachi

A. The Major Prophets

The first five books of prophecy are called major because they are longer than the other books, not because they are more important.

1. *Isaiah* lived in Jerusalem and was

an adviser of King Hezekiah. His book is a ringing call to righteousness, a clear warning of the captivity that would come because of sin, and a bright promise of restoration after the captivity. More than seven hundred years before Christ he foretold the Saviour so clearly that his book is sometimes called "the gospel according to Isaiah." Read Isaiah 53 and note the many details of Jesus' suffering and death.

2. *Jeremiah* lived in Jerusalem before and during the invasions that brought defeat and captivity. He too pointed out that captivity would come as a result of sin, and he too held out the promise of restoration. Note his promise of a new covenant in Jeremiah 31:31-34.

3. *Lamentations* was written by Jeremiah. In it he laments the fate of Jerusalem, but confesses that it was just punishment for her sins.

4. *Ezekiel* was one of the captives in Babylon. His book vividly rebukes the sins of the people and defends the justice of God.

5. *Daniel* also was one of the captives, but he became a trusted adviser of the Babylonian king. His book is notable for foretelling the great empires of Persia, Greece, and Rome that would follow the empire of Babylon.

B. Minor Prophets

The minor prophets are placed after the major prophets in the arrangement of the Bible, but Obadiah, Joel, Jonah, and Amos actually lived and taught earlier than any of the major prophets. Only Haggai, Zechariah, and Malachi came later than any of the major prophets.

1. *Hosea,* writing just before the fall of Israel, pictured God's loving forgiveness and pleaded with his people to repent, but his plea was unheeded.

2. *Joel* wrote a century earlier, but already he could see and denounce the sins that would finally lead to disaster.

3. *Amos* came from the country to urge the city dwellers to turn away from their selfishness, dishonesty, and cruelty.

4. *Obadiah* briefly foretold the destruction of Edom, an enemy nation.

5. *Jonah* carried God's call for repen- tance to a heathen city. There it was heeded even while it was ignored by God's chosen people.

6. *Micah* lived at the same time as Isaiah and brought a similar message. Through his book Jewish scholars knew Christ was to be born in Bethlehem (Micah 5:2; Matthew 2:1-6).

7. *Nahum* foretold the final ruin of Nineveh, the city that had repented a century and a half earlier at the preaching of Jonah, but had again fallen into sin.

8. *Habakkuk,* troubled because sinners were so long unpunished, asked God about it. The reply was that punishment may be slow by human standards, but it is utterly sure unless the sinners repent.

9. *Zephaniah,* shortly after Habakkuk, sounded another call for sinners to repent.

10. *Haggai* was one of the prophets who taught after his people returned to Jerusalem after the Babylonian captivity. He urged them to be diligent in building the temple and continuing faithful worship.

11. *Zechariah* lived at the same time as Haggai and brought a similar message.

12. *Malachi* was the last of the Old Testament prophets. His book closes with a prophecy that was fulfilled four hundred years later in John the Baptist, the forerunner of Jesus (Malachi 4:5, 6; Matthew 11:11-14).

C. The Prophets and Their Work

There were many more prophets besides those whose books are found in the Old Testament. Elijah and Elisha are among the most famous. Some prophets, like Isaiah, were trusted counselors of kings. Some, like Amos, were farmers who became preachers of righteousness. Some, like Elijah, were regarded as enemies by rulers who gladly would have killed them. But all of the prophets faithfully delivered the messages God gave them to deliver. All of them were authorized spokesmen for the Almighty, whether the message had to do with sin and righteousness in their own times or with events hundreds of years in the future.

25

QUESTIONS

1. Name the books of law.

_____

_____

_____

2. Name the books of history.

_____

_____

_____

_____

3. Name the books of poetry.

_____

_____

_____

_____

4. Name the books of prophecy.

_____

_____

_____

_____

_____

_____

_____

5. What is the meaning of the word *Genesis?*

_____

6. How could the writer of Genesis know what happened in the creation of the world before there were any people?

_____

_____

_____

7. What is the meaning of the word *Exodus?*

_____

8. Who were the Levites and what was their work?

_____

_____

_____

9. Name the major prophets.

_____

_____

_____

_____

10. What was the work of the prophets?

_____

_____

_____

_____

_____

Books of the New Testament

Lesson 5

The New Testament has twenty-seven books—three times three times three.

Review the four groups of New Testament books as given in Lesson 3.

THE GOSPELS

Probably you can name the Gospels.

The word "gospel" means "good news." Each of these books gives the good news that Jesus came to earth, died to save us from sin and death, and rose from the dead bringing "life and immortality to light" (2 Timothy 1:10).

Because they tell of the earthly life of Jesus, the Gospels are often called the *books of biography*.

The Gospels were written by the men whose names they bear. Matthew and John were two of the twelve apostles, eyewitnesses of Jesus' ministry. Mark may have known Jesus, and he almost certainly knew most of the apostles. Early Christian testimony indicates that Peter supplied most of the information given in Mark's Gospel. Luke is the one New Testament writer who probably was not Jewish. He probably spent two years in Palestine, collecting information from many eyewitnesses of Jesus' ministry and writing his record under the direction of the Holy Spirit.

Why are there four stories of the life of Christ instead of only one? Read the purpose of John's Gospel in John 20:31. No doubt the other Gospel writers had the same purpose. This purpose can be accomplished better by four writers, all guided by the Holy Spirit and all telling the same story, but telling it in different ways. Each writer has his own individual style, and each one may appeal more than the others to some readers. You may find that one of the Gospels is your own favorite, even though you treasure them all and find them helpful.

1. *Matthew* seems to have been written especially for Jews who knew the Old Testament and were looking for the Messiah. Often it points out the fulfillment of prophecy. See Matthew 1:22, 23; 2:1-6, 13-15, 16-18.

2. *Mark* is a short, vigorous record such as would appeal to the active Romans. Often prompt action is indicated by "straightway," "immediately," or "forthwith" (Mark 1:10, 12, 18, 20, 21, 28, 29, 31, 42).

3. *Luke* is a literary masterpiece such as would appeal to cultured Greeks like Luke himself.

Matthew, Mark, and Luke are called *Synoptic Gospels,* from Greek words meaning seeing together or seen together. They are so similar in viewpoint and content that they can be printed in parallel columns and seen together.

4. *John* was written perhaps thirty years after the Synoptic Gospels. It tells many of the same events, but concentrates on things not already told. John records more of the deep spiritual teaching of Jesus, such as that on the new birth (John 3:1-21), the bread of life (John 6:26-58), and the good shepherd (John 10:1-30).

THE BOOK OF HISTORY

Acts is the one book of history in the New Testament. Although often titled *The Acts of the Apostles,* it tells only *some* of the acts of *some* of the apostles. Written by Luke, a frequent companion of Paul, it tells more of the acts of Paul than of any other apostle.

By telling how people became Christians under the teaching of inspired men, Acts reveals how people may become Christians today (Acts 2, 8, 9, 10, 16). It also gives helpful records of the worship and life of Christians. For example, they continued in "the apostles' doctrine and fellowship, and in breaking of bread, and in prayers" (Acts 2:42). They took care of needy Christians (Acts 6:1-6). When they were driven from home, they went everywhere preaching the word (Acts 8:4).

THE LETTERS

The New Testament has twenty-one *letters.* Some prefer the name *epistles,* which means the same. Each one is named either for the writer or for the person or group of people to whom it was written.

A. Paul's Letters

The first fourteen letters probably were written by Paul, though no one really knows who wrote the fourteenth, Hebrews. These fourteen may be memorized in four groups—three, four, four, three.

Romans	Galatians
1 Corinthians	Ephesians
2 Corinthians	Philippians
	Colossians

1 Thessalonians	Titus
2 Thessalonians	Philemon
1 Timothy	Hebrews
2 Timothy	

B. Letters From Others

The remaining seven letters were written by four authors, and each is named for its writer. They are easily memorized in the following arrangement:

James	1 Peter	1 John	Jude
	2 Peter	2 John	
		3 John	

C. Other Designations

Paul's letters sometimes are called *special letters* because each is addressed to a special person, such as Timothy, or to a church in a specific place, such as Romans. Galatians is addressed to several churches in one area. Hebrews often is included in the group for the sake of convenience, even though it has no special address.

The remaining letters are called *general letters* because they are not addressed to any particular person or group. Second John and 3 John are exceptions, but are included in the "general" group for the sake of convenience.

Four of Paul's letters are called *prison epistles* or *captivity epistles:* Ephesians, Philippians, Colossians, and Philemon. Paul wrote these while he was prisoner, probably in Rome (Acts 28:16-31).

Three of Paul's letters are called *pastoral epistles:* 1 Timothy, 2 Timothy, Titus. These were written to help Timothy and Titus in guiding or shepherding Christian people. The word "pastor" literally means a shepherd.

THE BOOK OF PROPHECY

Revelation is the one book of prophecy in the New Testament. The writer was John the apostle. The book records the revelation Jesus gave him while he was in exile on the island of Patmos. Probably this was the last Bible book to be written. Its date may be shortly before A.D. 100. It pictures conflict between good and evil, but teaches the final victory of Christ and His people.

QUESTIONS

1. Name the four Gospels.

_____

_____

2. Why are we given four stories of Jesus' life instead of only one?

_____

_____

_____

_____

_____

3. Briefly tell some outstanding features or characteristics of each of the four Gospels.

_____

_____

_____

_____

_____

4. Who wrote the book of Acts?

_____

5. Tell something of the message and purpose.

_____

_____

_____

6. Name the New Testament letters with the writer of each.

_____

_____

_____

_____

_____

_____

_____

_____

_____

_____

_____

_____

_____

_____

_____

_____

_____

7. Who wrote the book of Revelation?

_____

8. Tell something of its message and purpose.

_____

_____

_____

_____

THE BIBLE LIBRARY

Book	Summary of content
Genesis	Beginning of the world, humanity, and the Hebrew nation
Exodus	Release of the Hebrew nation from captivity in Egypt
Leviticus	Laws of the priesthood
Numbers	Forty years in the wilderness
Deuteronomy	Reviewing the Law before entering the Promised Land
Joshua	Conquest of Canaan
Judges	First 300 years of the Hebrew nation in Canaan
Ruth	Beginning of the Messianic family
1 Samuel	The Hebrew nation becomes a kingdom
2 Samuel	The reign of David
1 Kings	The reign of Solomon and the separation of Israel and Judah
2 Kings	Last 130 years of Israel and last 250 years of Judah
1 Chronicles	Genealogies and the reign of David
2 Chronicles	Reign of Solomon and the history of Judah until captivity
Ezra	Return from captivity and the rebuilding of the temple
Nehemiah	Wall of Jerusalem rebuilt
Esther	Jews saved from extermination
Job	The problem of suffering
Psalms	Hymn and prayer book of the Hebrew nation
Proverbs	Wisdom about the practical affairs of life
Ecclesiastes	A debate about the meaning of life
Song of Songs	Glorification of marital love
Isaiah	Warnings to Judah and prophecies of the Messiah
Jeremiah	Warnings of the coming destruction of Judah
Lamentations	Poems by Jeremiah lamenting the fall of Jerusalem
Ezekiel	Prophecies to the Jews during the captivity
Daniel	The prophet Daniel in Babylon; Daniel predicts future events
Hosea	Israel described as God's unfaithful wife
Joel	Judah called to repentance after experiencing disaster
Amos	Wickedness of Israel condemned
Obadiah	The destruction of Edom
Jonah	An errand of mercy to the enemies of Israel
Micah	Impending fall of Israel and Judah
Nahum	The destruction of Nineveh foretold
Habakkuk	God to use Babylon to judge Judah
Zephaniah	Imminent judgment of Judah
Haggai	Encouragement to Zerubbabel to rebuild the temple
Zechariah	Encouragement to God's people rebuilding the temple
Malachi	Condemnation of priests and people who returned from captivity

Taken from *Old Testament Maps and Charts,* Standard Publishing, Cincinnati, Ohio. Used with permission.

THE BIBLE LIBRARY

Book	Summary of content
Matthew	Jesus the Messiah
Mark	Jesus the powerful servant of God
Luke	Jesus the Son of Man
John	Jesus the Son of God
Acts	History of the ministries of Peter and Paul
Romans	Justification by grace through faith
1 Corinthians	Solving problems in a selfish, sensual church
2 Corinthians	Joys of repentance, defense of Paul's apostleship
Galatians	Freedom in Christ
Ephesians	The glorious church
Philippians	Joy in Christ
Colossians	Christ is superior to any philosophy or religion
1 Thessalonians	Holy living and second coming of Christ
2 Thessalonians	Questions about the second coming of Christ
1 Timothy	How to lead a church
2 Timothy	Preaching the gospel in a hostile culture
Titus	Church maturity and church leadership
Philemon	Personal letter about forgiveness and fellowship
Hebrews	Superiority of Christianity over Judaism
James	Practical advice for faithful living
1 Peter	Enduring suffering
2 Peter	Teaching the truth
1 John	Assurance of salvation in the midst of false teaching
2 John	Warning against false teachers
3 John	Warning against false teachers
Jude	Warning against false teachers
Revelation	Ultimate victory of Christ and the church

Taken from *New Testament Maps and Charts*, Standard Publishing, Cincinnati, Ohio. Used with permission.

Three Dispensations

Lesson 6

A *dispensation* is a plan or way by which God dispenses or gives out His revelation, His blessing, and His punishment. Taking a broad view of all history, we see that God has dealt with mankind according to three great plans or dispensations. These may be given the following names:

Patriarchal
Jewish or Mosaic
Christian

THE PATRIARCHAL DISPENSATION

In the earliest ages of mankind, it is recorded that God revealed His will to some of the patriarchs. The word "patriarchs" means chief fathers.

A. Some of the Patriarchs

Among the chief ancestors to whom God gave revelations are Adam, Noah, and Abraham.

1. To *Adam* God gave a home, a task, and a prohibition, along with dominion over the rest of the earthly creation (Genesis 1:28, 29; 2:15-17).

2. To *Noah* God gave blessing and dominion and prohibitions and promise (Genesis 9:1-17).

3. To *Abraham* God gave a call, a home, and a promise (Genesis 12:1-3).

B. Patriarchal Worship

The *altar* was the institution of worship in patriarchal times. The offering of sacrifices began at least as early as Abel (Genesis 4:3, 4); perhaps Adam himself offered sacrifices. Noah and Abraham also built altars and made sacrifices (Genesis 8:20; 12:8), as did other patriarchs.

THE JEWISH OR MOSAIC DISPENSATION

A. Beginning of a New Dispensation

A new dispensation began when God gave the law to His chosen people, with a promise that they would be blessed when they obeyed and would be punished when they disobeyed. This is called the Jewish dispensation because the Jews were the chosen people who received the law. It is called also the Mosaic dispensation because God gave the law through Moses.

B. Jewish Worship

In the Jewish dispensation, worship centered in the *tabernacle,* in which the altar of sacrifice had a prominent place. Later the tabernacle was replaced by the *temple,* and still later the *synagogues* were added. These will be studied in a later lesson.

THE CHRISTIAN DISPENSATION

A. Extent of the Christian Dispensation

The earthly life and work of Jesus laid the foundation for a new dispensation. His death opened the way for the forgiveness of sins. This ended the dispensation of the Mosaic law. Soon afterward the new dispensation was announced on the Day of Pentecost, A.D. 30 (Acts 2). This dispensation will continue until the return of Jesus.

B. A Distinctive Feature

God now dispenses or gives salvation and blessing by His grace, not because we deserve them. Christians do try earnestly to do the Lord's will in everything; but they know they fail, and so depend on the Lord's forgiveness.

C. Christian Worship

The *church* is the institution of worship in the Christian dispensation. It replaces temple and tabernacle, and Christ's sacrifice of His life replaces the sin offerings made at the altar.

OTHER NAMES OF THE DISPENSATIONS

A. Promise, Law, Grace

1. The *patriarchal dispensation is* sometimes called *dispensation of promise* because of the promises made to the patriarchs.

2. The *Jewish* dispensation is known also as the *dispensation of law* because the law was given to guide the Jews.

3. The *Christian* dispensation is called the *dispensation of grace* because Christians rely on God's grace for their salvation.

B. Starlight, Moonlight, Sunlight

1. The *patriarchal* dispensation is called the *starlight dispensation* because the only divine revelation given to lighten the world consisted of the communications to the patriarchs.

2. The *Jewish* dispensation is called the *moonlight dispensation* because the revelation of God's law gave added light to guide mankind.

3. The *Christian* dispensation is called the *sunlight dispensation* because the revelation given through Christ and the apostles is far more complete and brilliant than the former revelations.

QUESTIONS

1. What is meant by a dispensation?

_____

_____

2. Name the three dispensations.

_____

_____

_____

3. Why are they sometimes called starlight, moonlight, and sunlight dispensations?

_____

_____

_____

_____

4. When did each dispensation begin and end?

_____

_____

5. What religious institutions of each dispensation can you name?

_____

_____

_____

STARLIGHT   MOONLIGHT   SUNLIGHT

PATRIARCHAL   JEWISH MOSAIC   CHRISTIAN

PROMISE   LAW   GRACE

The Old Testament World

Lesson 7

PHYSICAL FEATURES

A. Three Important Areas

Three areas are most important in Old Testament history: *Mesopotamia, Canaan, Egypt.* Locate them on Map 1. Practice till you can draw a rough outline of this map from memory and show these areas.

B. Three Less Important Areas

Locate three areas of less importance and learn to add them to your own drawing from memory:

1. The *desert* between Mesopotamia and Canaan. Most travelers went around this to the north.

2. *Syria,* between upper Mesopotamia and Canaan. This was on the usual route of travel.

3. The *peninsula of Sinai,* between Canaan and Egypt. There the Israelites spent forty years on their way to Canaan.

C. Four Rivers

Four rivers are prominent in the Old Testament: Tigris, Euphrates, Jordan, and Nile. Locate them. With the Jordan, locate the Sea of Chinnereth (pronounced *Kin*-ner-eth) and the Salt Sea. Give other names of these.

D. Three Bodies of Water

Locate three larger bodies of water:

1. *The Persian Gulf,* which does not enter into Old Testament history.

2. *The Red Sea,* crossed by the Israelites as they left Egypt.

3. *The Great Sea,* in which Jonah was swallowed by a big fish. What is its modern name?

E. Three Mountains

Locate three mountains that appear in Old Testament history.

1. *Mount Sinai,* where the law was given to Israel.

2. *Mount Nebo,* where Moses died at the border of the Promised Land.

3. *Mount Carmel,* where Elijah held his great contest with the prophets of Baal.

EMPIRES

Five peoples in turn held great power in the Old Testament world. Study Map 2 and learn where the homelands of these peoples were.

1. *Egypt* was a powerful nation in which the people of Israel were once guests and then slaves. At times it dominated Canaan and invaded Mesopotamia.

2. *Israel's empire* in the time of Solomon extended from the border of Egypt to the Euphrates. It was one of the most powerful empires of that time.

3. *Assyria* later conquered all of Mesopotamia and most of Canaan and Egypt.

4. *Babylonia* conquered Assyria and took all its territory. It destroyed Jerusalem and took most of the remaining Jews to Mesopotamia in captivity.

5. *Media and Persia* combined to take all this territory from Babylonia. They released the Jews from captivity, but continued to rule till the close of Old Testament history.

MT. ARARAT

TIGRIS R.

Haran

M E S O P O T A M I A

SYRIA

EUPHRATES R.

GREAT SEA

MT. CARMEL

CANAAN

JORDAN R.
MT. NEBO

Babylon

Ur

DESERT

PENINSULA
OF
SINAI

EGYPT

NILE R.

MT. SINAI

RED SEA

PERSIAN
GULF

0   100   200   300
MILES

MAP 1

ASSYRIA

MEDIA

ISRAEL'S EMPIRE

BA·BYLONIA

PERSIA

EGYPT

MAP 2

SPECIAL PLACES
AND EVENTS

1. *The Garden of Eden* was on the Tigris and Euphrates. Many students suppose it was where these rivers lie close together about the middle of their course. Find the place on your map. Some suppose the garden was at the end of the Persian Gulf. Find that place too.

2. We have no way of knowing how far mankind spread before the flood, but we are told that Noah's ark came to rest on *Mount Ararat* after the flood. Find the mountain.

3. Noah and his descendants evidently came down from the mountains into Mesopotamia. *The tower of Babel* is generally supposed to have been near where Babylon later arose. Find Babylon.

4. From Babel the people scattered in all directions. Later Abraham moved from *Ur* to *Haran* and then to *Canaan*. Trace his journey.

5. Joseph was taken from *Canaan* to *Egypt*, and his family followed later. Trace the trip.

6. Moses led his people out of *Egypt*, across the *Red Sea* to *Mount Sinai*. After wandering forty years in the *peninsula of Sinai*, they passed east of the *Salt Sea* and came to the east side of the *Jordan River*. Trace the journey.

QUESTIONS

1. Name the three areas most important in Old Testament history.

_____

_____

_____

2. Name three areas of less importance and tell where each was.

_____

_____

_____

_____

3. Name four rivers and tell which of the three important areas is associated with each river.

_____

_____

_____

_____

4. Name three bodies of water.

_____

_____

_____

5. Name three mountains and associate an event with each one.

_____

_____

_____

6. Name five nations that in turn held great power. In which of the important areas did each nation have its homeland?

_____

_____

_____

_____

_____

7. Name a place or event associated with each of these:

Garden of Eden _____

Tower of Babel _____

Joseph the slave _____

Mount Ararat _____

Haran _____

Old Testament People Part One

Lesson 8

Why study Old Testament history, since the old covenant has been replaced by the new? Because Old Testament history not only helps us understand God and the way of righteousness, but also provides background for the New Testament. New Testament writers frequently refer to Old Testament characters and events, and a knowledge of these enriches our knowledge of the New Testament.

SIXTEEN LEADING CHARACTERS

An outline of Old Testament history built around sixteen leading characters is easy to learn and remember. Memorize these names in four groups of four:

Adam	Moses	Saul	Isaiah
Noah	Joshua	David	Jeremiah
Abraham	Gideon	Solomon	Daniel
Joseph	Samuel	Elijah	Nehemiah

ASSOCIATED EVENTS AND PEOPLE

To make this list of names an outline of Old Testament history, learn to associate with each name a few other names and events recorded in the Old Testament.

1. Adam and the Creation

Along with Adam we think of the beginning of the world, mankind, sin, and punishment. But with punishment came the first promise of redemption (Genesis 3:15).

Associated with Adam are his wife *Eve* and his sons *Cain* and *Abel*.

2. Noah and the Flood

The first sin was by no means the last. As men became more numerous they became more wicked, and at last God determined to destroy all mankind except the one family still willing to serve Him. This was done by the great flood, through which Noah and his family were saved in the ark.

Associated with Noah are his three sons, *Shem, Ham,* and *Japheth.*

3. Abraham and the Chosen People

As mankind multiplied after the flood, wickedness again increased. This time God did not destroy all the wicked, but chose one godly man to become the head of a godly race that would be God's witness in a godless world and finally would bring the Saviour into the world. The man chosen as the father of this race was Abraham.

With Abraham we associate his nephew *Lot,* his son *Isaac,* and his grandson, *Jacob,* whose twelve sons became heads of the tribes of Israel.

4. Joseph and Egypt

Sold as a slave in Egypt, Joseph became a ruler and was able to save his father and brothers from starvation and give them a pleasant home. In later times, however, their descendants were oppressed and enslaved in Egypt.

With Joseph we associate his oldest brother *Reuben,* his youngest and favorite brother *Benjamin,* and *Pharaoh,* the chief ruler of Egypt.

5. Moses and Freedom

Moses, a Hebrew reared and trained in the palaces of Pharaoh, was chosen of God to lead the growing nation of the chosen people from Egypt back to Canaan, to give them God's law, and to write the books of law.

With Moses we associate *Pharaoh*, (not the one of Joseph's time, but a later ruler of Egypt who was an enemy rather than a friend); Moses' brother *Aaron*, who became the first high priest of Israel; and Moses' father-in-law, *Jethro*, a wise adviser.

6. Joshua and the Promised Land

Moses, a hundred twenty years old, died at the border of the Promised Land. Joshua led his people as they wrested the land from the heathen for their home.

With Joshua may be remembered *Caleb*, a faithful fellow soldier; *Eleazar*, Aaron's son who succeeded him as high priest; and *Rahab*, a friend in an enemy city.

7. Gideon and the Judges

After Joshua died, the chosen people often fell into sin and were punished by invasions of heathen people. Each time they repented of their sins, God gave a leader to help them drive out the invaders. These leaders were called judges, and Gideon was one of the most notable of them.

Besides Gideon we may remember *Samson*, the strong man; *Deborah*, the woman judge; and *Ruth*, a foreign woman who became an ancestress of Christ.

8. Samuel and a New Era

Samuel was the last of the judges. He anointed the first two kings of Israel, Saul and David.

With Samuel we may remember *Hannah*, his mother; *Eli*, the high priest who trained him; and *Joel* and *Abiah*, his wicked sons.

DISPENSATIONS

Review the dispensations presented in Lesson 6 and place each of these eight characters in the proper dispensation.

GEOGRAPHY

Use the map on page 35 and point out the area or areas associated with each of these eight characters.

QUESTIONS

1. Why should Christians, who are guided by the New Testament, study Old Testament history?

_____

_____

2. Name the first eight of the sixteen leading characters in this lesson, and mention at least one event and one other person associated with each.

_____	_____	_____
_____	_____	_____
_____	_____	_____
_____	_____	_____
_____	_____	_____
_____	_____	_____
_____	_____	_____
_____	_____	_____

Old Testament People

Part Two

Lesson 9

SIXTEEN LEADING CHARACTERS

Review the list of sixteen leading characters given in Lesson 8.

ASSOCIATED EVENTS AND PERSONS

Lesson 8 mentioned some events and persons associated with the first eight of the sixteen leading characters. This lesson deals with the remaining eight characters.

9. Saul, the First King

In Samuel's old age, the people asked for a king. God and Samuel did not approve, but they consented. The chosen king was Saul, who proved to be an able leader for a time and won some notable victories. But all too soon he began to ignore God's will and follow his own selfish inclinations. In time this led to his defeat and death.

With Saul we remember *Kish,* his father; *Jonathan,* his son who was a close friend of David; and *Abner,* Saul's great general.

10. David, the Great King

David was the second king of Israel. He defeated the surrounding heathen nations and made Israel the most powerful empire of the time. He was also a great musician, and many of the psalms are his work. Though notable sins are recorded against him, the main course of his life was so good that he is known as a man after God's own heart.

With David we may remember *Goliath,* the giant whom he slew;

Nathan, the prophet who rebuked his sin; and *Absalom,* his conceited son who led an armed-rebellion against him.

11. Solomon, the Wise King

Solomon, David's son and the next king, was especially gifted with wisdom. Proverbs, Ecclesiastes, and the Song of Solomon are evidences of this. He began his reign well, building a magnificent temple and adding glory to the great empire David had built. Later, however, he failed to follow the wisdom of his own inspired teachings. He taxed the people too heavily, and drafted them mercilessly for public works as well as for the army. He also married many heathen women and helped them introduce idolatry and wickedness into Israel. Because of his oppression and growing sin, his people were ready to revolt at the end of his reign.

With Solomon we may recall the *queen of Sheba;* Solomon's son *Rehoboam* who became the next king; and *Jeroboam,* king of the northern part of Israel that rebelled and became an independent nation.

12. Elijah, the Prophet

After the kingdom was divided, each section had many kings, but not many good ones. The rest of Old Testament history can be outlined better by using the names of great prophets. One of the greatest was Elijah, who boldly stood against the efforts of King Ahab and Queen Jezebel to turn the worship of

Israel from Jehovah to Baal. There is no book of Elijah, but his work is recorded in the two books of Kings.

With Elijah we associate *Jezebel,* the heathen queen; *Ahab,* the king who brought her from Phoenicia to be his wife; and *Elisha,* another prophet who was a helper and successor of Elijah.

13. Isaiah, the Gospel Prophet

We have come to a point in history about seven hundred years after Moses and seven hundred years before Christ. Isaiah prophesied when the northern part of Israel's split nation was taken into captivity. He foretold so many things about Christ and Christianity that he is called the gospel prophet.

With Isaiah we remember *Sennacherib,* the Assyrian king who tried to destroy the southern kingdom; *Hezekiah,* the good king of the southern kingdom who survived the attack of Sennacherib and for a time almost ended idolatry in the south; and Manasseh, the wicked son and successor of Hezekiah.

14. Jeremiah, the Weeping Prophet

Jeremiah lived when Jerusalem was destroyed and the remnant of the southern kingdom was taken into captivity. He foretold and lamented the captivity, but foretold also the later restoration and the new covenant.

With Jeremiah we may remember *Huldah,* prophetess who also foretold the fall of Jersualem; *Jehoiakim,* the wicked king who burned God's Word written by Jeremiah; and *Zedekiah,* the last king of the southern kingdom.

15. Daniel the Brave

Daniel was one of the Israelites taken to Babylon in captivity. With God's help, he became a trusted adviser to kings of Babylon and Persia. In mystic symbolism his book tells of great events to come.

With Daniel we associate *Nebuchadnezzar,* the Babylonian king who conquered the Old Testament world and made captives of the people of the Jews' southern kingdom; *Belshazzar,* last Babylonian ruler of Babylon, whose doom Daniel foretold; and *Cyrus,* the Persian king who conquered Babylon and freed the Hebrew captives.

16. Nehemiah the Restorer

Nehemiah was a governor of the Jews after they returned from captivity in Babylon. He rebuilt the walls of Jerusalem, reorganized its government, and restored respect for the law of God.

Associated with Nehemiah are *Artaxerxes,* Persian king who appointed Nehemiah as governor of Judah; *Ezra,* a scholar devoted to the teaching of God's law; and *Malachi,* who wrote the last Old Testament book about 400 B.C.

QUESTIONS

List eight leading characters in this lesson and mention at least one person and one event associated with each.

_____	_____	_____
_____	_____	_____
_____	_____	_____
_____	_____	_____
_____	_____	_____
_____	_____	_____
_____	_____	_____

40

Old Testament Periods Part One

Lesson 10

Old Testament history can be easily remembered in six natural periods. Commit these to memory:

1. Probation
2. Preparation
3. Conquest
4. Power
5. Decline
6. Servitude

This lesson deals with the first two of these periods. The remaining periods will be considered in Lessons 11 and 12.

PERIOD OF PROBATION

"Probation" means testing. In this early period man was tested to see whether he would obey God or not. Most of mankind failed the test, but Noah and his family passed the test and were saved. The period of probation extends from Adam to Noah, from the creation to the flood. It is recorded in the first nine chapters of Genesis.

A. Events of the Period of Probation
1. The *fall,* which brought sin into the world (Genesis 3:6).
2. The *promise of redemption,* which brought hope (Genesis 3:15).
3. The *deluge,* or flood, in which those who believed and obeyed God were saved (Genesis 7:11, 12).

B. Persons of the Period of Probation
1. *Adam,* with whom we associate the creation, fall, and promise of redemption.
2. *Noah,* with whom we associate the flood and the repeopling of the world.

PERIOD OF PREPARATION

As people became more numerous after the flood, sin again increased. This time God did not destroy mankind, but began the preparation of a special nation that would be His own, separated from the rest of the world. The period of preparation extends from Noah to Moses, from the flood to the exodus from Egypt. It is recorded in Genesis 10-50.

A. Events of the Period of Preparation
1. *The dispersion.* After trying to build the tower of Babel up to heaven, the people were dispersed or scattered, becoming separated tribes with different languages (Genesis 11:1-9).
2. *Journeys of the patriarchs.* Abraham moved from Ur to Canaan (Genesis 11:31—12:5); and in the time of his grandson Jacob, the family moved to Egypt (Genesis 45:1—46:7).
3. *Experiences in Egypt.* At first the chosen people were honored guests in Egypt (Genesis 47:1-12), but after a change in the government, they became mistreated slaves (Exodus 1). In the centuries in Egypt, the family of seventy increased to a nation of possibly three million.

B. Persons of the Period of Preparation
1. *Abraham,* who trusted God and became the forefather of the chosen people.
2. *Joseph,* who was sold as a slave, became ruler of Egypt, and gave a home to his people in their time of need.

41

First period	Events	Persons

Second period	Events	Persons

QUESTIONS

1. In the first column above, put the names of the first two periods of Old Testament history.

2. In the second column, list three events of each period.

3. In the third column, write the names of two persons of each period.

4. Explain why the period of probation is so called.

_____

_____

_____

_____

_____

5. Explain why the period of preparation is so called.

_____

_____

_____

_____

_____

REVIEW

1. Since we do not have any Bible books in the handwriting of the original writers, what ancient documents help us be sure the Bible of today is nearly the same as the original writings? (Lesson 1).

_____

2. Give some simple rules to follow in Bible study (Lesson 2).

_____

_____

_____

3. Without writing them, name the divisions of Old and New Testaments and name the books in each (Lessons 3, 4, 5).

4. Name the three great dispensations, giving at least two names of each (Lesson 6).

_____

_____

_____

The Conquest of Canaan

Conquests Under Moses ············
Conquests Under Joshua ─ ─ ─ ─ ─

Mediterranean Sea

Sidon

Great Sidon

Tyre

Dan

Kadesh

Waters
of Meron

Merom

Hazor

BASHAN

Ashtaroth

Edrei

Megiddo

GILEAD

Shechem

SAMARIA

Jordan River

Shiloh

Adam

Jazer

AMMON

Ai

JERICHO

Gilgal

Beth-horon

AMMORITES

Heshbon

Gezer

Makkedah

Gibeon

Plains
of Moab

PHILISTIA

JERUSALEM

Jahaz

Azekah

Libnah

Lachish

Eglon

Hebron

DEAD SEA

Gaza

Debir

Arad

MOAB

Hormah

N E G E B

E D O M

Kadesh-barnea

Taken from *Old Testament Maps and Charts*, Standard Publishing, Cincinnati, Ohio. Used with permission.

43

Old Testament Periods Part Two

Lesson 11

Review the six periods of Old Testament history. This lesson continues the study of them.

PERIOD OF CONQUEST

With the help of God, His people broke away from Egypt, crossed the desert, and conquered Canaan.

The period of conquest extends from Moses to Samuel, from the exodus to the end of the judges' time. It is recorded in the Old Testament books from Exodus to 1 Samuel. Review the names of these.

A. Events of the Period of Conquest

1. *Experiences in the wilderness.* After ten plagues had persuaded Pharaoh to set them free, the people of Israel crossed the Red Sea into the wilderness. There they received the law from God, built the tabernacle as He commanded, and wandered for forty years before entering the Promised Land (Exodus, Leviticus, Numbers, Deuteronomy). Follow their journey on page 35.

2. *Conquest of Canaan.* Like the people who lived before the flood, the heathen of Canaan had now become so utterly wicked that they must be destroyed. God chose to use the people of Israel for this purpose. At His command, Joshua led them as they conquered the land (book of Joshua). However, they failed to destroy or drive out the heathen as completely as God had ordered, and the remaining heathen troubled them often in later centuries.

3. *Rule of the judges.* The law given at Mount Sinai was still the law of Israel, but after Joshua died there was no national government to enforce it. Enforcement by tribes or families was not consistent, and often "every man did that which was right in his own eyes" (Judges 17:6). When most of the people became wicked, God allowed enemies to invade their land and rob them. When they gave up their wrongdoing and kept the law, God gave them a leader to guide them in defeating the enemies. Fifteen such leaders, called judges, are mentioned in the book of Judges.

B. Persons of the Period of Conquest

1. *Moses* led Israel from Egypt to the border of the Promised Land.

2. *Joshua* led in driving out the heathen and taking their land.

3. *Gideon* was one of the judges.

4. *Samuel* was the last of the judges. After defeating the invaders, he acted as a sort of governor for years.

PERIOD OF POWER

Under the rule of its earthly kings, Saul, David, and Solomon, Israel developed a strong central government and became the most powerful nation of the time. The period of power reached from Samuel to Solomon, from the crowning of Saul to the division of the nation after the death of Solomon. It is recorded in 1 and 2 Samuel and eleven chapters of 1 Kings.

A. Events of the Period of Power

1. *Saul's defeat* by the Philistines and his death (1 Samuel 31:1-13).

2. *David's capital* was established at Jerusalem. There he placed the sacred

When David was king, Israel conquered and ruled the other countries named on the map.

David's son, Solomon, therefore ruled an empire reaching from the river of Egypt to the Euphrates.

EUPHRATES R.

SYRIA

ISRAEL

PHILISTIA

JUDAH

MOAB

AMMON

EDOM

RIVER OF EGYPT

After Solomon died, ten of the twelve tribes revolted and the kingdom was split. The ten northern tribes kept the name of Israel, while Judah and Benjamin together were called Judah.

The conquered nations then regained their independence, and even took some of the territory of Israel.

ark of the covenant (2 Samuel 5:1-10; 6:12-19).

3. *Solomon's temple* at Jerusalem replaced the tabernacle as the home of the ark and the center of Israel's worship (1 Kings 6).

B. Persons of the Period of Power

1. *Saul,* the first king of God's chosen people.

2. *David,* the warrior king who built an empire.

3. *Solomon,* the last king of the united kingdom.

QUESTIONS

1. In the first column below, write the names of the first four periods of Old Testament history.

2. In the second column, write three events of each period.

3. In the third column, write the names of two persons of the first period, two of the second period, four of the third period, and three of the fourth.

A REMINDER: Have you sent for the test questions?

First period	Events	Persons

Second period	Events	Persons

Third period	Events	Persons

Fourth period	Events	Persons

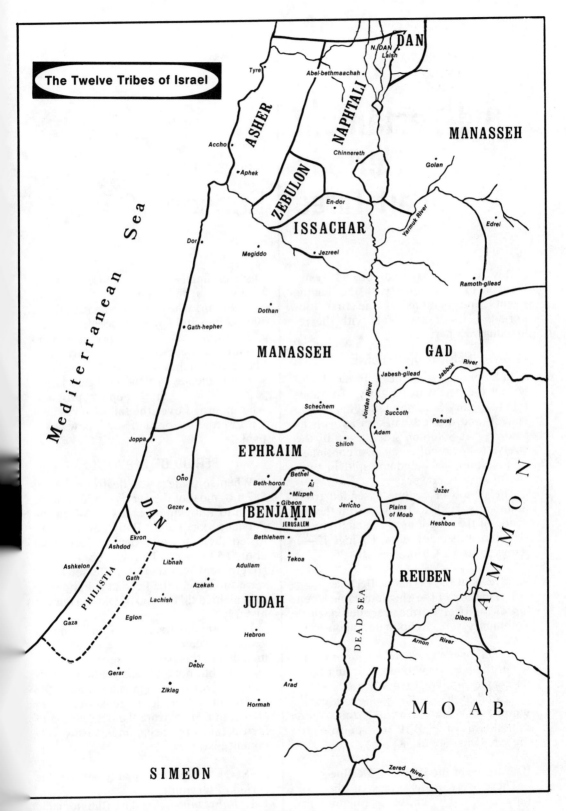

The Twelve Tribes of Israel

Mediterranean Sea

Tyre
N. DAN
Laish
DAN
Abel-bethmaachah
ASHER
NAPHTALI
MANASSEH
Accho
Chinnereth
Golan
Aphek
ZEBULON
En-dor
ISSACHAR
Yarmuk River
Edrei
Dor
Megiddo
Jezreel
Ramoth-gilead
Dothan
Gath-hepher
MANASSEH
GAD
Jabbok River
Jabesh-gilead
Schechem
Jordan River
Succoth
Penuel
Joppa
Shiloh
Adam
EPHRAIM
Ono
Bethel
Beth-horon
Ai
Mizpeh
Jazer
Gezer
Gibeon
Jericho
Plains of Moab
BENJAMIN
JERUSALEM
Heshbon
DAN
Ekron
Bethlehem
Ashdod
Ashkelon
PHILISTIA
Libnah
Adullam
Tekoa
REUBEN
Gath
Azekah
AMMON
Lachish
JUDAH
DEAD SEA
Gaza
Eglon
Dibon
Hebron
Arnon River
Gerar
Debir
Arad
Ziklag
M O A B
Hormah

SIMEON
Zered River

Taken from *Old Testament Maps and Charts*, Standard Publishing, Cincinnati, Ohio. Used with permission.

Old Testament Periods
Part Three

Lesson 12

Review the six periods of Old Testament history, together with the leading events and persons of the first four periods. This lesson deals with the remaining two periods.

PERIOD OF DECLINE

In Solomon's time the empire of Israel was at the height of its glory. To maintain that glory Solomon taxed his people heavily and drafted workers as well as soldiers. At Solomon's death ten of the twelve tribes revolted against continued oppression. The kingdom, split in two, swiftly lost its power.

The period of decline extended from Solomon's death to Daniel, from the division of the kingdom to the captivity in Babylon. It is recorded in 1 Kings 12—2 Kings 25 and 2 Chronicles 10—36.

A. Events of the Period of Decline

1. *Division* of the kingdom came when ten of the twelve tribes rebelled against Solomon's son, Rehoboam, about 930 B.C.

2. *End of the northern kingdom* came when the Assyrians overran it and took its people captive about 721 B.C.

3. *Fall of the southern kingdom* came when the Babylonians destroyed Jerusalem and took its people to Mesopotamia about 587 B.C.

B. Persons of the Period of Decline

There were many kings of the two kingdoms, but we chose to remember instead three prophets who tried to prevent the decline and fall of the kingdoms.

Disaster finally came because their advice was not followed.

1. *Elijah,* who opposed the idolatry of King Ahab and Queen Jezebel.

2. *Isaiah,* the gospel prophet, who foretold the captivity and return, and also told much about the Saviour who would come seven hundred years later,

3. *Jeremiah,* the weeping prophet, who mourned over the fall of Jerusalem but foretold restoration and a new covenant.

PERIOD OF SERVITUDE

When Jerusalem was destroyed about 587 B.C. most of the surviving Jews were taken to Babylon as captives. When the Persians conquered Babylon, they allowed the Jews to return to Jerusalem about 536 B.C. Though some self-government was allowed, the Jews still were subjects of the Persian Empire, and so remained till the end of Old Testament history.

For convenience, the four hundred years between the testaments are also included in this period of servitude. During most but not all those years the Jews were subject to foreign rulers. Thus the period of servitude is reckoned from Daniel to Christ, from the destruction of Jerusalem to the beginning of New Testament history.

A. Seven epochs are readily seen in the period of servitude.

1. *Babylonian rule.* The Babylonians, also called Chaldeans, held the Jews in the Bablylonian captivity from 587 B.C.

48

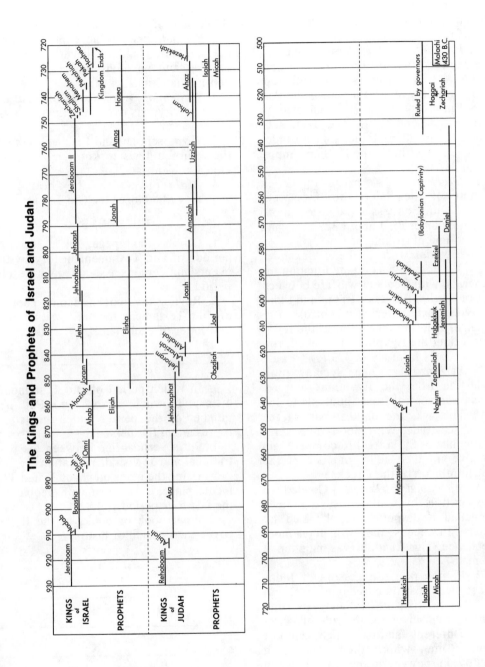

The Kings and Prophets of Israel and Judah

Taken from *Old Testament Maps and Charts*, Standard Publishing, Cincinnati, Ohio. Used with permission.

49

until their empire was taken over by the Persians about 538 B.C.

2. *Persian rule.* The Persians allowed the captive Jews to return to Jerusalem and govern themselves, but still kept them and their land as a part of the Persian Empire. This Persian rule was in force at the end of the Old Testament about 400 B.C. It continued till Alexander the Great overthrew the Persian Empire about 332 B.C.

3. *Greek rule.* As a part of the Greek Empire of Alexander, the Jews were treated with kindness and consideration. But Alexander died about 323 B.C., and then a time of trouble began.

4. *Egyptian rule.* When Alexander died, his empire was divided among his generals, with frequent warfare between various parts. Rulers of Egypt and those of Syria fought bitterly for control of Canaan, or Palestine, the home of the Jews. For a time the Egyptians prevailed, ruling the Jews from about 323 to 204 B.C.

5. *Syrian rule.* The Syrians took Palestine from the Egyptians and remained in control from about 204 to 167 B.C. This was the darkest part of the Jews' servitude. With bloody massacre, Antiochus of Syria tried to compel them to give up their faith and accept the pagan religion of the Greeks.

6. *Maccabean freedom.* Goaded to desperation by Antiochus, the Jews launched a desperate revolt. Led by Judas Maccabeus, they won their independence. This freedom was maintained from 167 to 63 B.C.

7. *Roman rule.* Successors of Judas Maccabeus lost their religious zeal and became selfish politicians, battling among themselves for the rule of Palestine. Different factions sought support from Rome, which then was rising swiftly in power. In 63 B.C. Pompey moved into Jerusalem, and the Jews came under Roman rule, which continued into New Testament times. Jesus was born during the reign of Herod, whom the Roman emperor appointed as king of the Jews. By the calendar we now use, the birth of Jesus was about 5 B.C.

B. Persons of the Period of Servitude

1. *Daniel,* one of the captives from the southern kingdom, became a great prophet and an adviser of Babylonian and Persian kings.

2. *Nehemiah,* governor of Judea after the captivity was over, rebuilt the walls of Jerusalem.

3. *Ezra,* scholar and teacher, helped the returned Jews to know and follow God's ancient law.

4. *Malachi* wrote the book of prophecy that closes the Old Testament.

QUESTIONS

1. On the next page, fill in the six periods of Old Testament history, with events and persons associated with each period.

2. Review the sixteen leading people of Old Testament history, writing the first letter of each name on this line.

_____

3. In which period of Old Testament history did each person live? Put the number of the period under the letter representing the person.

4. Put a vertical line between the patriarchal and Jewish dispensations.

5. Using the maps on pages 35 and 47, locate places associated with people of the last four periods.

6. What book or books of the Bible cover each period of history?

1. _____

2. _____

3. _____

4. _____

5. _____

6. _____

7. Using maps on pages 35, 47, and 94, locate the following and tell of their part in history: Assyria, Babylonia, Persia, Greece, Egypt, Syria, Rome.

First period	Events	Persons

Second period	Events	Persons

Third period	Events	Persons

Fourth period	Events	Persons

Fifth period	Events	Persons

Sixth period	Events	Persons

Altar and Tabernacle

Lesson 13

In Old Testament times, group worship centered in three memorable institutions: the altar, the tabernacle, and the temple. The altar was the institution of the patriarchal dispensation. The tabernacle was added in the Jewish dispensation. Later it was replaced by the temple. A fourth institution, the synagogue, came into being near the end of Old Testament times after the Israelites had been taken into captivity.

THE ALTAR

The *altar* is a symbol of *sacrifice,* which had an important place in Old Testament worship.

A. The Beginning of Sacrifice

It is quite possible that sacrifice began with Adam, but the first recorded sacrifices are those of Cain and Abel (Genesis 4:3-5). No altar is mentioned in this record, but the place of offering, however simple, may be considered an altar.

B. How Altars Were Made

Perhaps the simplest altar was but a mound of earth on which sacrifices were burned. The custom of the Hebrew patriarchs, Abraham, Isaac, and Jacob, was to build a rough stone altar wherever they camped. While the Israelites were in the wilderness after leaving Egypt, they made an altar of wood and brass or bronze that could be carried with them in their wanderings. This was placed in the courtyard of the tabernacle. When a permanent temple was built, there was a massive altar of natural stone in its courtyard.

C. Use of the Altar

Sacrifices of various kinds were burned in a wood fire on the altar. They may be divided into two classes:

1. *Sacrifices made to atone for sin and seek forgiveness.* Among these were the burnt offerings, sin offerings, and trespass offerings. Such sacrifices have been replaced by the sacrifice of Christ to atone for the sins of the world.

2. *Sacrifices made to express thanksgiving, devotion, and fellowship with God.* Among these were the peace offering and the meat offering. (The meat offering was of meal or baked bread. In the old English of our Bible, "Meat" means food of any kind.) With a similar purpose the Christian presents his body a living sacrifice in unselfish living and service (Romans 12), offers praise to God (Hebrews 13:15), and gives sacrificially to those in need (Hebrews 13:16).

THE TABERNACLE

When the people of Israel came out of Egypt, they were ready to begin their life as an independent nation. At Mount Sinai God gave them the law they were to live by. He gave also instructions for building a tabernacle to symbolize His dwelling among His people and to serve as a center of worship.

A. Materials of the Tabernacle

The Hebrew word for tabernacle is the common word for a tent. The tabernacle was God's tent in the midst of the tents of His people. Like the tents of the people, it could be easily taken down and moved. This was necessary because the nation was just starting on its long journey to the Promised Land.

The walls of the tabernacle were of fabric over a wooden frame. The roof was of fabric and skins. The fence around the large court was of fabric supported by wooden posts. Nevertheless, the structure was costly, symbolizing the willing devotion of God's people. Fabrics were richly embroidered; wooden parts were covered with gold, silver, or brass. The people had brought these precious materials out of Egypt with them (Exodus 11:2; 12:35, 36).

B. Plan of the Tabernacle

God gave Moses directions for building the tabernacle and warned him to follow the directions exactly (Exodus 25:9). No doubt one reason for such care was that the tabernacle was to be a symbol of the church that was to come centuries later (Hebrews 8:1, 2; 10:1). Details of the symbolism are not given in Scripture (Hebrews 9:5), but are generally taken to be as suggested below.

1. *The court* or yard about the tabernacle measured 150 feet by 75. It is taken as a symbol of the world.

2. *The altar of burnt offering* was seven and a half feet square and four and a half feet high. Sacrifices were burned upon it, symbolizing the sacrifice of Christ for the sins of the world.

3. *The laver* was a large basin where the priests washed their hands and feet before going into the Holy Place. It is a symbol of Christian baptism.

4. *The Holy Place,* 30 by 15 feet, symbolized the church separated from the world (the court) and entered by ways of Christ's sacrifice (the altar) and baptism (the laver).

5. *The table of shewbread,* on which twelve loaves were placed every week, was a symbol of the Lord's Supper.

6. The *candlestick,* more properly a lamp stand holding seven lamps, gave light for the Holy Place. Thus it was a symbol of God's Word, which enlightens the church.

7. *The altar of incense* provided a place where incense was burned. The sweet-smelling smoke ascended like the prayers of God's people.

8. *The veil* was a curtain between the Holy Place and the Most Holy Place. It symbolized the separation between heaven and the Christians on earth.

9. *The Most Holy Place,* perfect cube fifteen feet long, wide, and high, was a symbol of heaven, the particular place of God's presence.

10. *The ark of the covenant* was a wooden chest covered with gold and having a golden lid bearing two golden cherubim. The ark contained the Ten Commandments symbolizing God's government; a dish of manna, recalling God's providence; and Aaron's rod, a reminder of God's power among His people (Hebrews 9:4). Once a year the high priest sprinkled the top of the ark with blood, a symbol of Christ's blood by which we are cleansed.

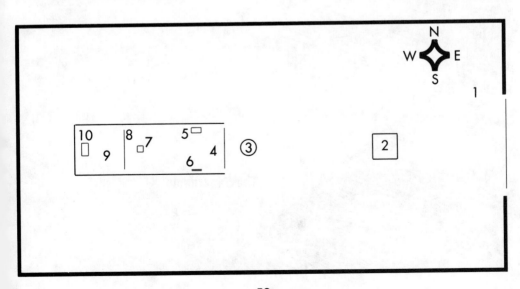

QUESTIONS

1. Which of the institutions named in this lesson belonged to the patriarchal dispensation?

_____

2. Of what materials were altars made?

_____

3. Give the two classes of offerings mentioned in the lesson and tell what there is in the Christian dispensation to correspond to each.

_____

_____

_____

_____

4. When and where did God give instructions for building the tabernacle?

_____

5. Why was the tabernacle building portable?

_____

_____

6. Name ten parts of the tabernacle and furnishings, and tell what each may symbolize.

_____

_____

_____

_____

_____

_____

_____

_____

_____

_____

The Tabernacle

Temple and Synagogue | Lesson 14

THE TEMPLE

For about five hundred years, from the time of Moses to the time of Solomon, the tabernacle was Israel's place of worship. During this time the people left their tents and occupied well-built villages and cities in the Promised Land. After Jerusalem became the capital city, David thought of building a temple there to replace the tabernacle. After David's death, his son Solomon directed the building of the temple David had planned. This temple later was replaced by others, but all of them were built on the same site and all had at their center a reproduction of the tabernacle with the Most Holy Place and the Holy Place.

A. Three Temples

1. *Solomon's temple* was finished about 960 B.C. Its ground plan was the same as that of the tabernacle; but the measurements were doubled, and the building was made of stone and cedar instead of fabrics. This temple stood nearly four hundred years before it was destroyed by Nebuchadnezzar's men.

2. *Zerubbabel's temple* was built between 536 and 516, after the Israelites returned from captivity in Babylon. Zerubbabel was the governor of Jerusalem who directed the work. His temple was at least as large as Solomon's, but probably not so richly adorned with gold. It lacked the ark of the covenant, which probably had been destroyed by the Babylonians. This temple was not destroyed as the first one was, but after five hundred years it was thoroughly rebuilt by Herod the Great, who ruled in Palestine when Jesus was born.

3. *Herod's temple* was the result of the rebuilding program begun by Herod about 20 B.C. To avoid a general destruction of the old temple, the rebuilding was done a little at a time. It took only a year and a half to complete the temple itself, reproducing the form of the ancient tabernacle. But work on the surrounding buildings went on for years. The whole structure was not completed until about A.D. 64, only six years before the Romans finally destroyed it. During the

ISRAEL'S THREE TEMPLES		
Solomon's Temple	Zerubbabel's Temple	Herod's Temple
Built 960 B.C.	Built 536-516 B.C.	Built 20 B.C.-A.D. 64
Destroyed 586 B.C.	Rebuilt 20 B.C.-A.D. 64	Destroyed A.D. 70

ministry of Jesus it was said that the temple had been forty-six years in building (John 2:20).

B. Plan of Herod's Temple

Since Herod's temple was the one we read about in the New Testament, we should know something about the plan of it, which of course was similar to that of the earlier temples.

1. The Most Holy Place and the Holy Place still preserved the shape of the original tabernacle, though they had the larger size of Solomon's temple. At the east end of the Holy Place an elaborate porch rose high in the air. On the other three sides there were rooms, probably used by the priests for various purposes.

2. Around this central structure was the Court of Priests, enclosing the laver and the big altar at which the priests offered sacrifices.

3. Around the Court of Priests was the narrow Court of Israel in which the men of Israel brought their sacrifices to the priests.

4. East of this court was the Court of Women, about three hundred feet square, where both men and women of Israel gathered for their group worship. Around the outside of this court were rooms for meetings or for storage.

5. Outside of this was the large Court of Gentiles, nearly nine hundred feet square. This court was open to anyone, Jewish or foreign. This was where Jesus found the merchants selling sheep, cattle, and doves that might be offered in sacrifice. Along the walls were roofed areas, or porches, where people and animals could find shelter from rain or sun. At the northwest corner was a stronghold where soldiers were quartered, ready to put down any riot or rebellion that might arise when throngs gathered in the court.

THE SYNAGOGUE

A. Origin and Purpose

The synagogue probably began during the Babylonian captivity when the temple was in ruins. Unable to go to Jerusalem to worship, the Jews kept their ancient faith alive by meeting for worship and teaching in the various towns where they were forced to live. There was only one temple for the whole nation, but each community could have a synagogue, just as each community now can have a local church. Synagogues are mentioned frequently in the New Testament.

CASTLE ANTONIA

COURT OF ISRAEL

COURT OF

MOST HOLY PLACE

HOLY PLACE

Altar

PRIESTS

Laver

COURT OF WOMEN

Beautiful Gate

Steps

SOLOMON'S PORCH

SACRED INCLOSURE

COURT OF GENTILES

N
W E
S

ROYAL PORCH

HEROD'S TEMPLE

Study this plan and practice until you can draw it roughly from memory. Do not try to memorize details; simple lines are enough to indicate the temple and the various courts.

The model pictured on page 56 is located in the grounds of the Holyland Hotel in Jerusalem. Compare it with the plan above and identify the various courts. The picture is taken as if we were looking toward the temple from the southeast.

The large fortress you see directly to the north of the porticoes is the Antonio Fortress. Herod named this after Mark Antony. The fortress was connected to

the temple by staircases. It is believed that this fortress is where Paul was taken when arrested in the temple (Acts 21).

You may see small differences between model and plan. We cannot be sure of all details because descriptions of the temple are incomplete. The sanctuary was built of three kinds of marble. The two columns in front were of reddish marble in memory of the two that stood in front of Solomon's temple. The rest of the building was of white marble with a foundation of blueish stones. Josephus described the temple as resembling "a snowy mountain glittering in the sun."

B. Uses of the Synagogue

1. The synagogue was a *Bible school* where the Scriptures were taught.

2. It was a *house of worship* for the Sabbath and other occasions.

3. It was a *day school* in which children were taught the Scriptures along with reading and writing.

C. Officers of the Synagogue

1. Each community had a council of elders known as *rulers of the synagogue*. They directed the services, and also acted as town council and court.

2. The *ministers* helped with the services, took care of the buildings, and sometimes were schoolteachers.

3. The *batlanim* (bat-lah-*neem,* men of leisure) were men who had some leisure time to give to the affairs of synagogue and community.

QUESTIONS

1. How was Israel's temple like the tabernacle?

_____

_____

2. How was the temple different from the tabernacle?

_____

_____

_____

3. At the top of the three boxes below, write the names of the builders of Israel's three temples.

4. Below each name, write the approximate date when this man built.

5. Next write who destroyed or rebuilt that temple. Add D for destroyed or R for rebuilt.

6. At the bottom of the box, put the approximate date when the temple came to an end.

7. Explain when and why the synagogue came into being.

_____

_____

_____

_____

_____

_____

8. What uses were made of the synagogue?

_____

_____

9. Name some officers of the synagogue.

_____

_____

The Jewish Feasts

Lesson 15

SOME GENERAL THOUGHTS

A. Importance of the Jewish Feasts to us.

1. The New Testament has many references to Jewish feasts. Knowing about them helps us fix the time of the year and understand what is going on. For example, Jesus was crucified at the Passover, and the church began its work at Pentecost.

2. The feasts commemorate events that are as dear to Christians as to Jews. The escape from Egypt and the giving of the law are part of the preparation for the gospel.

B. Names of the Feasts

1. There were three great feasts: Passover, Pentecost, and Tabernacles.

2. There were three lesser feasts: Trumpets, Dedication, and Purim.

C. Two Calendars of the Jews

1. In patriarchal times, the Israelites considered that the year ended when the last of the fruits were gathered in the fall, and the new year then began with the fall plowing and planting. The first month corresponded nearly to October.

2. When the Israelites left Egypt, God said the month of their liberation should be the first month. In the Bible, the months are numbered on that basis, so the first month corresponds to April and the seventh month to October. However, the older calendar continued to be used in many civil and personal affairs, and the Jewish New Year still is celebrated in the fall.

THE GREAT FEASTS

A. Passover

1. The Passover was celebrated at the end of the fourteenth day of the first month and the beginning of the fifteenth. (The new day began at sunset.) It began the week-long feast of unleavened bread, and the whole week came to be known as the Passover.

2. The Passover originated when the Israelites were liberated from Egypt. Just before they left, God passed over the land to bring death to the first-born of every Egyptian home, but He passed over the Israelites without harm.

3. Each family had a lamb for the ceremonial Passover dinner; or two or more small families might share a lamb. This feast came just before the barley harvest, and the first sheaf of the harvest was one of the offerings. After the temple was built, the nation gathered there for the feast.

B. Pentecost

1. The Greek word *pentecostoas* means fiftieth. Pentecost was the fiftieth day after the Passover Sabbath. It is also called the feast of Weeks, because it came seven weeks after the Passover.

2. According to Jewish tradition,

Pentecost is the anniversary of the giving of the law at Sinai.

3. After the temple was built, the people of Israel gathered there for Pentecost. Barley and wheat were harvested between Passover and Pentecost, so thanksgiving was a feature of the second feast. This was symbolized by an offering of loaves of bread.

C. Tabernacles

1. The feast of Tabernacles began on the fifteenth of the seventh month (about October) and lasted one week.

2. This feast commemorated the years of wandering in the wilderness. To remind them of those wilderness days, the people left their houses and lived in temporary shelters made of branches. These were called tabernacles, and that name was given to the feast.

3. This feast was called also the feast of ingathering, because it came after all the fruits of the year had been gathered in. In a way it corresponded to our Thanksgiving.

D. The Three Lesser Feasts

1. *The feast of Trumpets* came on the first day of the seventh month. It was New Year's Day by the ancient patriarchal calendar. Modern Jews call it *Rosh Hashanah,* the beginning of the year.

2. *The feast of Dedication* called *Hanukkah* in the Hebrew language, was a week-long festival beginning on the twenty-fifth of the ninth month. It was known also as the feast of lights from the lamps and torches used to symbolize the light of liberty. This festival had its beginning in the time between the Old Testament and the New, when the temple was purified and rededicated after invading Syrians had defiled it.

3. *Purim* fell on the fourteenth and fifteenth of the twelfth month. It commemorated Queen Esther's deliverance of her people from the massacre planned by Haman. The name Purim means lots, recalling that Haman cast lots to decide when he would destroy the Jews (Esther 3:7).

E. The Day of Atonement

The Day of Atonement was the tenth of the seventh month. It was not a feast day, but a day of fasting and penitence. Special offerings were made to atone for sins.

QUESTIONS

1. Name the three great feasts of the Jews.

_____

_____

_____

2. What event was commemorated by the Passover feast?

_____

3. Give one New Testament event that took place at Passover time.

_____

4. Why was Pentecost so called?

_____

_____

5. What was commemorated by the feast of Tabernacles?

_____

6. What was one distinctive feature of the Tabernacle celebration?

_____

_____

7. Name three lesser feasts and tell what each commemorated.

_____

_____

_____

_____

_____

_____

8. What was the Day of Atonement?

_____

_____

FEASTS OF THE JEWS

Name	Designation	Month in Which Observed	Month of Sacred Year	Month of Civil Year	English Month Nearly	Duration of Feast	Where Observed	Main Feature of Its Observance	What It Commemorated	Other Names
Passover	Greater Feast	Nisan or Abib	1	7	April	One Week	Jerusalem	Eating paschal lamb	Passing over of death and departure from Egypt	Unleavened Bread
Pentecost	Greater Feast	Sivan	3	9	June	One Day	Jerusalem	Offering two loaves, representing first-fruits of wheat	Giving the law at Mt. Sinai	Weeks Firstfruits Wheat Harvest
Tabernacles	Greater Feast	Tisri or Ethanim	7	1	October	One Week	Jerusalem	Living in booths	Life in the Wilderness	Ingathering
Trumpets	Lesser Feast	Tisri or Ethanim	7	1	October	One Day	Anywhere	Blowing of trumpets	New Year's Day	
Dedication	Lesser Feast	Chisleu	9	3	Dec.	Eight Days	Anywhere	Rejoicing, singing, lighting of lamps and torches	Rededication of temple after recapturing it from heathen	Lights
Purim	Lesser Feast	Adar	12	6	March	Two Days	Anywhere	Reading Book of Esther	Queen Esther's rescue of the Jews	

Between the Testaments

The Old Testament canon closed with the restoration of the Jews to their homeland under the direction of Cyrus of Persia. They returned with high expectations for the Golden Age of Israel to be restored once more. But the years came and went to be met only with hardship, deprivation, and difficulty. Three significant tasks were completed—restoring the Temple, rebuilding the city walls, reestablishing the law community—but the restoration of old Israel was not to be realized.

The nearly four hundred years between the Testaments was not all peace and quiet, merely waiting for the coming of Jesus. Neither was it a time of unprecedented fidelity to the law of God. Rather it was another of those periods of tension with the surrounding culture and subsequent compromise with the pagan forces that played upon them.

RISE OF ALEXANDER

Persia dominated the world until 334 B.C. The Persian Empire extended over what is now Iraq, Iran, Lebanon, Israel, Jordan, Egypt, Turkey, parts of Greece, the Balkans, Soviet Russia, Afghanistan, and Pakistan. But those in the West weren't content for Persian control to continue. One—Alexander of Macedon—proposed to do something about it.

Young Alexander had studied under Aristotle who was an expert in the study of political institutions. Aristotle had once said, "The Greeks might govern the world, could they combine into one political society." That possibility became Alexander's dream.

Alexander's forces crossed the Hellespont in 334 B.C., a signal to the world that Hellenization was underway. The commander was but nineteen years old at the time. In four short years—by 330 B.C.—he captured the world and reportedly wept because there was no more to conquer.

Alexander the Great died in 323 B.C., and the kingdom went to an unborn son. Practically, however, it was divided into four areas under four generals. Two are of particular interest.

Seleucus provided oversight to Mesopotamia and Syria. The center was at Antioch. Ptolemy ruled Egypt, and the center was at Alexandria. An intense power struggle ensued—and Palestine was caught in the middle as usual. Late in the fourth century B.C., Palestine fell to the Ptolemies who ruled for a hundred years.

The Ptolemies permitted a great deal of autonomy to their subjects. Although Hellenization was a part of their program, it was not pursued vigorously. The Jews were permitted to practice their unique religion. (Even so, the priesthood was far from pure.)

RISE OF THE SELEUCIDS

In 198 B.C., Antiochus III, a Seleucid, claimed Palestine and crushed the Ptolemies. In many ways, he inherited a unified world, at least from a surface view. Oriental civilizations had destroyed themselves. The Jews had begun to speak Greek. (The Old Testament was even translated into Greek in the mid-200's B.C. It was called the Septuagint.) In 175 B.C., Antiochus Epiphanes ascended the throne. This brought uneasy matters to a head, for he began an aggressive Hellenizing campaign and imposed heavy taxation.

The collision course was hastened when this Antiochus proclaimed himself the epiphanes (the visible incarnation of Zeus) and demanded that he be worshipped. That was too much for faithful Jews. He also sold the high priesthood to Jason who was the highest bidder. The Jews were repressed.

In 168 B.C., Antiochus Epiphanes marched on Jerusalem. He took the city and celebrated by offering swine's flesh on the altar of the Temple and suspended the practice of Judaism. He forbade observance of the Sabbath and circumcision. Many Jews capitulated, but others didn't—and were severely mistreated.

RISE OF THE MACCABEES

Mattathias was one Jew who refused to capitulate to Antiochus' demands. He and his sons were able to lead a revolt by which temple worship was restored. Mattathias died very soon, and his son Judas Maccabees (the Hammer) led the continuing revolt.

Judas caused Antiochus to back off and defeated several regional powers. Over a three-year period he brought a semblance of peace. He was of the Hasmonean House from which came the high priests for many years thereafter. However, the high priests became corrupt and more than willing to accommodate to heathen practices. I Maccabees reports the wars and problems of the period. Intrigue followed intrigue, and religious motivations were frequently secondary.

RISE OF ROME

In 63 B.C., Palestine fell to Roman rule when Pompey led his forces against the Hasmonean House. The Herodians were appointed as puppet rulers and maintained oversight from B.C. 63 - A.D. 135. The first was Antipater who was succeeded by another Antipater and he by his son Herod the Great who ruled B.C. 37 - 4.

Herod the Great was a wild, passionate, unbending, cunning man of insatiable ambition. During his period of prosperity, B.C. 25 - 13, he rebuilt the Temple, built cities, theaters, and other extravagant buildings, introduced Roman culture, and curried Roman friendship to the dismay of the Pharisees. His latter years were spent with domestic discord and slander. By the time of the birth of Jesus, his position was shaky which, perhaps, explains, in part, his reaction to the report of the birth of Jesus.

Herod died in 4 B.C., and his kingdom was divided three ways. Archelaus ruled Judea from 4 B.C. - 6 A.D. Herod Antipater governed Galilee from 4 B.C. - 39 A.D. Philip took control of Iturea from 4 B.C. - 34 A.D.

RELIGIOUS DEVELOPMENTS

By the time the New Testament canon was opened, Judaism subscribed to the centrality and authority of the Torah, observed the sacrificial services of the Temple, and believed that God's Kingdom would center in Palestine. But party differences had arisen over *how* these tenets of faith should be interpreted.

The Sadducees came from the priestly families. They claimed strict adherence to the Torah—so strict that they rejected the doctrine of the resurrection because they found no evidence for it in the Torah. Yet, because they were interested in the priestly *status quo*, they advocated a degree of compromise with Hellenism, *if* the Temple services were to continue.

On the other hand, the Pharisees, the largest and most influential group, practiced strict separatist practices: dietary rules, circumcision, fasting, prayer. They wanted nothing to do with Gentiles. Yet, they accepted teachings of books in addition to the Torah and added a body of oral tradition called the Talmud.

The Zealots were closely related to the Pharisees in doctrine. However, they were political activists who were much like the Maccabean revolutionaries.

The Essenes were a radical order who totally withdrew from society. Their zeal for the Torah and for the apocalyptic kingdom led them to become an ascetic, celibate community of strict discipline as they awaited the coming of the Kingdom.

The center of worship became the synagogue. Wherever ten men could be found to form a congregation, synagogues were created as a center of prayer, worship, and instruction. Feasts still had to be observed in the Temple, but the synagogue assumed centrality for social and educational life.

It was to this world, united under Roman rule, yet divided by competing philosophies, that Jesus came. It was within this Jewish party system that Jesus revealed the essence of God, though the party people generally missed it. It was in the midst of this religious confusion that the New Testament era emerged.

New Testament Lands

Lesson 16

Nearly all of the earthly life of Jesus was spent in Palestine, a little area east of the Mediterranean Sea. Acts and the letters of the New Testament bring us to other lands east and north of the Mediterranean.

PALESTINE

A. Study the map on the opposite page and practice until you can sketch a rough outline map of Palestine with four lines, two down and two across.

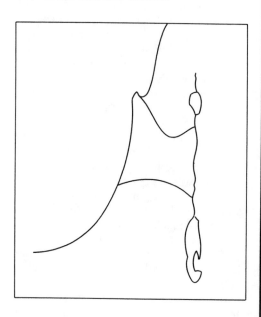

1. *The Mediterranean coast*. Note the one small jog about one third of the way from the top.
2. *The Jordan River*. Place the Sea of

Galilee opposite the jog in the coast line, the Dead Sea at the bottom of the map.
3. Learn to place the boundary between *Galilee and Samaria*.
4. Finally, locate the boundary between *Samaria and Judea*. Note that it meets the Jordan about one third of the way up from the Dead Sea to the Sea of Galilee.
5. Learn the names of six large areas, three on each side of the river. It is especially important to be well acquainted with those on the west side, since they are named more frequently in the four Gospels.
B. Learn to locate four towns and cities from memory.
1. *Jerusalem,* the capital. Place it directly west of the north end of the Dead Sea.
2. *Bethlehem,* where Jesus was born, six miles south of Jerusalem.
3. *Nazareth,* where Jesus lived in His youth. Place it directly west of the south end of the Sea of Galilee.
4. *Capernaum,* often called Jesus' headquarters during His ministry. Locate it on the northwest shore of the Sea of Galilee.
C. Make it a habit to locate on the map each place you find in your study of the Scriptures. For practice, mark the following places on the map on the opposite page.
1. *The place where a man was beaten by robbers and helped by a good Samaritan* (Luke 10:30-36). You cannot locate it

SYRIA

Sidon

Damascus

Zarephath

PHOENICIA

Tyre

Caesarea Philippi

TETRARCHY OF
PHILIP

Capernaum

Bethsaida

Cana

Gergesa

GALILEE

Nazareth

Bethabara

Caesarea

DECAPOLIS

SAMARIA

Sychar

○JACOB'S
WELL

Joppa

PEREA

Jericho

Jerusalem

Bethany

Azotus

Bethlehem

JUDEA

●Gaza

0   10   20   40

Scale   of   Miles

NABATEANS

65

exactly, but you can place it somewhere along a twenty-mile road between two cities named in the Scripture.

2. *The place where Jesus fed the five thousand.* Jesus and His apostles went there by sea (John 6:1). It was "a desert place," that is, uninhabited pasture land, near Bethsaida (Luke 9:10) and opposite Capernaum (John 6:17).

D. Using the scale of miles, estimate the following distances and write them on the lines provided.

1. The shortest distance from Nazareth to Jerusalem.

_____

2. The distance from Nazareth to Jerusalem by the route usually used. This avoided the country of the unfriendly Samaritans by crossing the Jordan near Bethabara, traveling south on the east bank, crossing the river again east of Jericho, and then climbing the mountain road to Jerusalem.

_____

OTHER NEW TESTAMENT LANDS

A. Study the map on the opposite page.

1. *You can easily learn* to sketch a very crude outline of this map from memory. See the sample below. Your

sketch may be even less accurate, but practice till you can reproduce the general shape of the outline that is shown.

2. *If you habitually look up* the location of every place named in the Scriptures you study, you will learn to visualize this map and know most locations without looking them up. To begin with, locate four cities.

a. The place where the book of Acts begins (Acts 1:4).

b. The place where the book of Acts ends (Acts 28:16).

c. The place where disciples were first called Christians (Acts 11:26).

d. The place to which Paul wrote 1 and 2 Corinthians (1 Corinthians 1:2; 2 Corinthians 1:1).

B. Paul made three notable missionary journeys starting from Antioch, and later made a voyage from Caesarea to Rome. Using the Bible record and the map on the opposite page, trace one or more of these trips.

1. *His first missionary journey* (Acts 13:1—14:28).

2. *His second missionary journey* (Acts 15:35—18:22).

3. *His third missionary journey* (Acts 18:23—21:15).

4. *His voyage to Rome* (Acts 27:1—28:16).

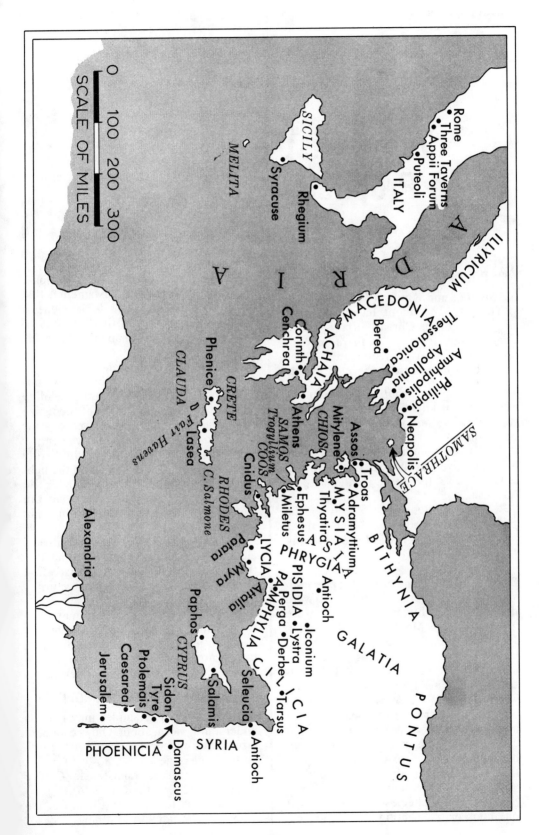

SCALE OF MILES
0 100 200 300

Rome
• Three Taverns
• Appii Forum
• Puteoli
ITALY

A D R I A

ILLYRICUM

SICILY
• Syracuse
Rhegium

MELITA

MACEDONIA
Thessalonica
Berea •
Amphipolis
Apollonia
Philippi •
Neapolis •
SAMOTHRACE

ACHAIA
Corinth •
Cenchrea •
Athens •

CRETE
Phenice •
CLAUDA
Lasea •
Fair Havens
C. Salmone
RHODES
Cnidus •
COOS •
SAMOS
Trogyllium
Miletus •
Ephesus •
Thyatira •
MYSIA
Mitylene •
Adramyttium
Assos •
Troas •

CHIOS

BITHYNIA

PONTUS

PHRYGIA

LYCIA
Patara •
Myra •
Attalia •
PAMPHYLIA
Perga •
PISIDIA
Antioch •
Iconium •
Lystra •
Derbe •
GALATIA
Tarsus •
CILICIA

Paphos •
CYPRUS
Salamis •
Seleucia •
Antioch •

Alexandria •

Jerusalem •
Caesarea •
Ptolemais •
Tyre •
Sidon •
PHOENICIA
Damascus •
SYRIA

The Christ in Prophecy

Lesson 17

PROPHECIES OF THE CHRIST

A. Number and Kinds of Prophecies

The Old Testament has very many prophecies of the Christ. Perhaps no one can tell how many, for there may be some that are not yet recognized. Three kinds of prophecies may be mentioned.

1. *Types or symbols*. For example, every animal killed in sacrifice may be regarded as a symbol of Christ's sacrifice of His life.

2. *Obscure prophecies*. Such was the early promise that the seed of the woman would bruise the head of the serpent (Genesis 3:15).

3. *Plain statements*. Such was the promise that God would raise up a prophet similar to Moses (Deuteronomy 18:15).

B. Writers and Time of the Prophecies

1. The prophecies about Christ were not all written by one man, but were given through Moses, David, Isaiah, Jeremiah, Daniel, Micah, Malachi, and others.

2. These prophecies were not all written at the same time. Those of Moses were written nearly fifteen hundred years before Christ came, those of David about a thousand years before Christ came, those of Isaiah more than seven hundred years before Christ came, and those of Malachi about four hundred years before Christ came.

3. These prophecies are not in just one book or one section of the Old Tes-tament, but run through all its sections. The first one in the Old Testament is that of the seed of the woman in Genesis 3:15; the last is that of the Sun of righteousness in the last chapter of Malachi.

C. Difficulty of Understanding

Prophecies about the Christ were understood so poorly that the leading scholars of His people did not recognize Him when He came. Some reasons for failure to understand are easily seen.

1. *Obscure prophecies* could hardly be understood well until seen in the light of their fulfillment. Such are the prophecies of the seed of the woman in Genesis 3:15 and the seed of Abraham in Genesis 22:18.

2. *The time element* was not always clear. For example, sometimes no distinction was made between Christ's first coming in humility and His later return in glory.

3. *Selfish wishes* of readers may keep them from understanding. Many Jewish students loved the prophecies of glory, but ignored or misunderstood the prophecies of humility and suffering.

SPECIFIC EXAMPLES OF PROPHECY

Study of a few examples may help us understand more about Old Testament prophecies concerning the Christ. Look up these passages.

1. Jesus was to minister in Galilee (Isaiah 9:1, 2; Matthew 4:12-16).

2. He was to enter Jerusalem in triumph (Zechariah 9:9; Matthew 21:4, 5).

3. He was to be despised and rejected (Isaiah 53:3; Matthew 27:21-23).

4. He was to be a man of sorrows (Isaiah 53:3; Matthew 26:36-38).

5. He was to be betrayed by a friend (Psalm 41:9; John 13:18).

6. Even the price was foretold (Zechariah 11:12, 13; Matthew 27:3-10).

7. He was to be silent on trial (Isaiah 53:7; Matthew 27:12-14).

8. He was to be sentenced to death (Isaiah 53:8; Mark 14:61-64; 15:15).

9. He was to suffer abuse (Isaiah 53:5, 7; Matthew 26:67, 68; 27:27-30).

10. He was to be scourged (Isaiah 53:5; John 19:1).

11. His hands and feet were to be pierced (Psalm 22:16; John 20:20, 25, 27).

12. His garments were to be shared by a lot (Psalm 22:18; John 19:23, 24).

13. He was to be numbered with transgressors (Isaiah 53:12; Mark 15:27, 28).

14. He was to endure cruel mockery (Psalm 22:7, 8; Matthew 27:41-43).

15. No bone was to be broken (Psalm 34:20; John 19:36).

16. He was to be pierced (Zechariah 12:10; John 19:37).

17. He was to be with the rich in His death (Isaiah 53:9; Matthew 27:57-60).

CONCLUSION

It is not to be believed that men by human power alone could look hundreds of years into the future and foretell such details accurately. But God guided the prophets, and God knows the future as well as the past.

QUESTIONS

1. Mention several kinds of prophecies about the Christ.

_____

_____

2. Name several men who wrote prophecies about the Christ. Add the approximate date if you can.

_____

_____

_____

_____

3. What is the first prophecy of Christ in the Old Testament?

_____

_____

4. What is the last prophecy of Christ in the Old Testament?

_____

_____

_____

5. Give some reasons that prophecies sometimes are not understood.

_____

_____

_____

_____

_____

6. Give a few details of Christ's life that were foretold in the Old Testament.

_____

_____

_____

_____

_____

_____

7. What conclusion is drawn from a study of these prophecies?

_____

_____

69

Life of Christ
Part One
Lesson 18

INTRODUCTORY WORD

A. New Testament History as a Whole

New Testament history naturally divides into three periods:
1. Life of Christ
2. Beginnings of the church
3. Work of Paul and John

B. Time of These Periods

1. *The earthly life of Christ* was from about 5 B.C. to A.D. 30. Date of His birth is about 5 B.C. by our calendar because a mistake was made when this calendar was first started. The makers of the calendar thought Jesus was born later than He really was.

2. *The beginnings of the church* include the years from A.D. 30 to 45, during which the gospel spread from Jerusalem through Judea and Samaria, reached to the Gentile Cornelius at Caesarea, and won many Gentiles to Christ in Antioch. Locate these places on the maps on pages 65 and 67.

3. *The work of Paul and John* reaches from about A.D. 45 to 100. Paul began his first missionary journey about 45; John finished his writing and his life about 100.

C. Periods in the Life of Christ

The earthly life of Christ may be divided into seven periods:
1. Thirty years of youth—preparation.
2. First year of ministry—obscurity.
3. Second year of ministry—popularity.
4. Third year of ministry—opposition.
5. Last three months—persecution.
6. Last week—"passion week."
7. Forty days—Jesus' appearances and instructions after His resurrection.

This lesson and the two following ones will deal with these seven periods of the life of Christ.

THIRTY YEARS OF YOUTH PERIOD OF PREPARATION

Memorize five events of the first thirty years of Jesus' life: *Birth, Flight, Return, Baptism, Temptation.*

1. *Birth* (Luke 2:1-20). Jesus was born in Bethlehem, a small town about six

PERIODS OF NEW TESTAMENT HISTORY

PERIOD	TIME	WHERE TOLD
Life of Christ	5 B.C.-A.D. 30	Gospels
Beginnings of the Church	A.D. 30-45	Acts 1—12
Work of Paul and John	A.D. 45-100	Acts 13—28
		Letters
		Revelation

miles south of Jerusalem, though the home of Joseph and Mary was in Nazareth, several days' journey away. Prophecy was fulfilled when He was born in Bethlehem (Micah 5:2), born of a virgin (Isaiah 7:14), and descended from Abraham, Judah, and David.

2. *Flight* (Matthew 2:1-15). When King Herod heard a new king had been born in Bethlehem, he determined to kill the child. Instructed by an angel, Joseph took the baby Jesus and His mother and fled to Egypt. Herod's slaughter of the other babies of Bethlehem fulfilled prophecy. See Jeremiah 31:15; Matthew 2:16-18.

3. *Return* (Matthew 2:19-23). When Herod died, Joseph and Mary brought Jesus back from Egypt and returned to their home in Nazareth, again fulfilling prophecy (Hosea 11:1; Matthew 2:15). Of Jesus' youth we know only one other event—His trip to Jerusalem at the age of twelve, where He amazed the scholars with His knowledge. After that He "increased in wisdom and stature, and in favour with God and man." See Luke 2:40-52.

4. *Baptism* (Matthew 3:1-17). John the Baptist, forerunner of Jesus, was preaching repentance and baptizing people "unto repentance" in preparation for the coming Christ. He was baptizing in the Jordan River east of Jerusalem.

Jesus came to be baptized, not because He had many sins to repent of, but in order to "fulfill all righteousness." Immediately after His baptism, "the heavens were opened unto him, and he saw the Spirit of God descending like a dove, and lighting upon him: and lo a voice from heaven saying, This is my beloved Son, in whom I am well pleased." This was the first public announcement that Jesus was God's Son.

5. *Temptation* (Matthew 4:1-11). Following His baptism, Jesus was led into the wilderness to be tempted of the devil, but He resisted every temptation. He is one who has been "in all points tempted like as we are, yet without sin" (Hebrews 4:15).

FIRST YEAR OF MINISTRY PERIOD OF OBSCURITY

Memorize five events from the first year of Jesus' ministry: *First Miracle, First Cleansing, Nicodemus, Woman of Samaria, Nobleman's Son.*

1. *First miracle.* In Cana of Galilee, not far from His home and probably in the home of a kinsman or friend, Jesus turned water into wine (John 2:1-11).

2. *First cleansing of the temple.* John 2:13-16 tells how Jesus cleansed the temple for the first time. He cleansed it again a few days before His death. By driving out the merchants and money changers, He made the temple what it was designed to be—a place of prayer.

3. *Nicodemus* was a scholar and ruler who came to Jesus by night and heard the first recorded discourse of our Lord. In it is the well-loved John 3:16. Read the rest in John 3:1-21.

4. *Woman of Samaria.* Weary from travel and waiting for His dinner, Jesus forgot His own needs to give His attention to a woman of a despised race and bad reputation. Here is a sample of personal evangelism (John 4:1-21).

5. *Nobleman's son.* Jesus healed this son without even going near him, giving us a remarkable demonstration of Jesus' power and the nobleman's faith (John 4:46-54).

John is the only book that tells us much about this period of obscurity.

Thirty Years—Preparation
Birth
Flight
Return
Baptism
Temptation

First Year—Obscurity
First Miracle
First Cleansing
Nicodemus
Woman of Samaria
Nobleman's Son

QUESTIONS

1. On the lines below, list three periods into which the whole of New Testament history may be divided. Give approximate dates for the beginning and end of each period. Tell where in the Bible we find information about each period.

_____   _____   _____

_____   _____   _____

2. List seven periods in the life of Christ, giving the approximate length of each period and a word describing it.

_____

_____

_____

_____

_____

_____

3. List five events of the preparation period. Tell something about each one.

_____

_____

_____

_____

4. List five events of the first year of Jesus' ministry. Tell a little about each one.

_____

_____

_____

_____

_____

Life of Christ
Part Two

Lesson 19

Review the first two periods of Jesus' life, recalling five events in each. If necessary, refresh your memory by looking at Lesson 18.

SECOND YEAR OF MINISTRY
PERIOD OF POPULARITY

Very many events of this year are recorded. Memorize five typical ones:
1. The calling of the fishers
2. The Sermon on the Mount
3. The widow's son
4. The lakeside parables
5. Jairus' daughter

1. *The calling of the fishers* (Matthew 4:18-22). Simon Peter, Andrew, James, and John were busy commercial fishermen whom Jesus called to follow Him. At that time multitudes of people were thronging about Him to see His miracles and hear His teaching. Besides the four fishers, He chose eight more to form the circle of twelve apostles.

2. *The Sermon on the Mount.* To His chosen twelve and a great multitude, Jesus set forth the basic principles of life in His kingdom. In this sermon we find the well-known Beatitudes and the Lord's Prayer (Matthew 5, 6, 7).

3. *The widow's son.* As Jesus was going about Galilee to teach and heal, He met a funeral procession coming out of the town of Nain. The dead man was a widow's son, and probably her only source of support. Jesus restored him to life (Luke 7:11-17).

4. *The lakeside parables.* Matthew 13 records eight parables that Jesus seems to have told in one day. At least part of them were told by the Sea of Galilee near Capernaum, while Jesus sat in a boat and spoke to the people on the beach. Can you tell in your own words the parables of the sower, the tares, the mustard seed, the leaven, the treasure in the field, the pearl of great price, the net, the householder?

5. *Jairus' daughter.* In Capernaum Jesus raised Jairus' daughter from the dead (Matthew 9:18-26; Mark 5:21-43). Jairus was a man of prominence, and the fame of this miracle spread everywhere, although Jesus asked that no one be told.

THIRD YEAR OF MINISTRY
PERIOD OF OPPOSITION

The common people heard Jesus gladly, but many scholars and rulers opposed Him. Their opposition was due partly to jealousy and partly to their anger at His rebukes of their sins and hypocrisy.

Memorize five of the many recorded events of this period:
1. Feeding the five thousand
2. Syrophoenician's daughter
3. Peter's confession
4. The transfiguration
5. The good Samaritan

1. *Feeding the five thousand* (Matthew 14:13-21). All four Gospels record this miracle. Jesus borrowed five loaves and two fishes from a boy and used them to feed five thousand men besides women and children.

73

2. *Syrophoenician's daughter* (Matthew 15:21-28). Withdrawing from the crowds of Galilee to have more time with His apostles, Jesus went northwest to the vicinity of Tyre and Sidon. Use the map on page 65 to locate that area. There He healed the daughter of a foreign woman, though His mission at that time was mainly to the people of Israel.

3. *Peter's confession* (Matthew 16:13-17). Many people supposed Jesus was a prophet, but His chosen twelve were convinced that He was the Christ, the Son of God. Peter voiced this belief in an impressive way and received a blessing in return.

4. *The transfiguration* (Matthew 17:1-8). A week after Peter's confession, Jesus took three disciples and sought solitude for a time on a high mountain. There He was transfigured, His face and His garments becoming a gleaming white. Before the eyes of the three disciples, Moses and Elijah appeared and talked with Jesus about His coming sacrifice of His life. Peter suggested building three shelters for Jesus, Moses, and Elijah; but the voice of God said, "This is my beloved Son, in whom I am well pleased; hear ye him."

5. *The good Samaritan* (Luke 10:29-37). The well-known good Samaritan is one of the finest examples of neighborliness. Nevertheless this story must have intensified the leaders' opposition to Jesus, for it pictured a despised Samaritan in more favorable light than two of their religious leaders.

QUESTIONS

1. In review, list the seven periods of Jesus' life that were named in Lesson 18.

_____

_____

_____

_____

_____

_____

2. In the spaces below, name four periods of Jesus life and list five events in each period. (Two periods were considered in the last lesson and two in this lesson.)

First period _____

_____

_____

_____

_____

_____

Second period _____

_____

_____

_____

_____

_____

Third period _____

_____

_____

_____

_____

_____

Fourth period _____

_____

_____

_____

_____

_____

Convincing Proofs of the Resurrection:

Scripture	Jesus appeared to	What senses were involved?	Other significant facts
Mark 16:9-11; John 20:11-18	Mary Magdalene	Sight, Hearing, Touch	Mary had to be convinced
Matthew 28:9, 10	Women	Sight, Hearing, Touch	More than one person involved
Mark 16:12, 13; Luke 24:13-32	Two on the way to Emmaus	Sight, Hearing	Jesus ate with them
Mark 16:14; Luke 24:36-43; John 20:19-25	The disciples	Sight, Hearing	They had to be convinced; there were several there; Jesus ate with them
John 20:26-31	The disciples, especially Thomas	Sight, Hearing, maybe Touch	The doubter believed
John 21:1-23	Seven disciples	Sight, Hearing	Jesus performed a miracle; He ate with them
Matthew 28: 16-20	Several disciples	Sight, Hearing	Doubters believed
Mark 16:15-20	Disciples	Sight, Hearing	His promise was fulfilled
Luke 24:44-49; Acts 1:3-8	Disciples	Sight, Hearing	Disciples learned new information
1 Corinthians 15:5-8	Cephas (Peter), the apostles, 500 brethren, James, the apostles, Paul		Many people saw him, Paul's whole life was changed.

Taken from *New Testament Maps and Charts,* Standard Publishing, Cincinnati, Ohio. Used with permission.

Life of Christ
Part Three

Lesson 20

Quickly review the first four periods of Jesus' life, mentioning five events in each period.

We now go on with the last three periods.

THE LAST THREE MONTHS
PERIOD OF PERSECUTION

Some of the rulers had thought of killing Jesus before this, but now they were plotting against His life more actively and vigorously.

Memorize five events of these three months.

1. Raising of Lazarus
2. Ten lepers healed
3. Little children
4. Rich young ruler
5. Zacchaeus

1. *Raising of Lazarus.* (John 11:1-16). About two miles from Jerusalem, just over the Mount of Olives, was the home of Mary, Martha, and Lazarus. It seems that Jesus was at home whenever He came there. Lazarus died; but after he had been in the tomb four days Jesus raised him from death.

2. *Ten lepers healed* (Luke 17:11-19). Leprosy was seldom cured. On this occasion Jesus healed ten lepers, and only one was grateful enough to return and thank Him.

3. *Little children* (Matthew 19:13-15). Knowing that Jesus was overworked, His disciples would have sent away the children who had come to see Him. But Jesus said, "Suffer little children, and forbid them not, to come unto me: for of such is the kingdom of heaven." No doubt this is partly responsible for the care we give to children in our Sunday schools.

4. *Rich young ruler* (Luke 18:18-27). A rich young ruler of fine character came to Jesus to ask about eternal life. Jesus made it very clear that one who would have eternal life must follow Him at all costs.

5. *Zacchaeus* (Luke 19:1-10). A rich tax collector, too short to see over the heads of other people, climbed into a sycamore tree to see Jesus pass. His earnest zeal was rewarded when Jesus went to his home, and the tax collector resolved to be honest and generous.

THE LAST WEEK
PASSION WEEK

Memorize five events of the week that ended with Jesus' death:

1. Mary's anointing
2. Triumphal entry
3. Ten virgins
4. Upper room
5. Crucifixion

1. *Mary's anointing.* Jesus was a supper guest in Bethany when Mary anointed Him with costly ointment (Matthew 26:6-13; Mark 14:3-9; John 12:1-8). Probably this was on Friday or Saturday a week before His death.

2. Triumphal entry (Matthew 21:1-11; Mark 11:1-11; Luke 19:29-44; John 12:12-16). On the first day of the week, Jesus entered Jerusalem as a king might enter in triumph, riding a young ass while the people waved palm branches and sang praises.

3. *Ten virgins* (Matthew 25:1-13). As

He taught in the temple on Tuesday, Jesus gave the parable of ten virgins to warn the people to be ready for His return.

4. *The upper room* (Matthew 26:17-29; Mark 14:12-25; Luke 22:7-38; John 13:1—17:26). In an upper room in Jerusalem Jesus ate the last supper with His disciples, and there He instituted the Lord's Supper. Probably this was Thursday night.

5. *Crucifixion* (Mark 14:53—15:39). On false accusations and perjured testimony Jesus was condemned to death, tortured, and nailed to a cross. In the midst of cruel taunts and terrible suffering, He prayed for His murderers and remembered to provide a home for His mother. Then He died for the sins of the world.

THE FORTY DAYS
RESURRECTION APPEARANCES

During the forty days between His resurrection and His ascension, Jesus appeared to disciples at least ten times.

Memorize five of them:
1. Appearance to two
2. Appearance to ten
3. Appearance to seven
4. Appearance to five hundred
5. Appearance to eleven

1. *Appearance to two.* Jesus joined two disciples as they walked to Emmaus (Mark 16: 12, 13). He had already been seen by Mary Magdalene.

2. *Appearance to ten.* All the eleven apostles except Thomas were together when Jesus appeared in their midst (Luke 24:36-48). Later He appeared to the group when Thomas was present.

3. *Appearance to seven.* By the Sea of Galilee Jesus had breakfast with seven apostles (John 21:1-14).

4. *Appearance to five hundred.* First Corinthians 15:6 tells us that Jesus was seen by more than five hundred brethren at once.

5. *Appearance to eleven.* Jesus met the eleven apostles in Galilee and commissioned them to take His gospel to the whole world (Matthew 28:16-20). Possibly it was at the same time that He was

seen by five hundred. He appeared again to the eleven at the time of His ascension (Luke 24:50, 51).

QUESTIONS

1. Name the last three of the seven periods of Jesus' life and list five events of each period.

Fifth period _____

_____

_____

_____

_____

_____

Sixth period _____

_____

_____

_____

_____

_____

Seventh period _____

_____

_____

_____

_____

2. In review, list three periods into which the whole of New Testament history may be divided. If you cannot recall them, refer to lesson 18 and fix them in memory.

_____

_____

_____

	PERIODS	EVENTS
Y O U T H	**Thirty Years—Preparation**	Birth Flight Return Baptism Temptation
M I N I S T R Y	**First Year—Obscurity**	First Miracle First Cleansing Nicodemus Woman of Samaria Nobleman's Son
	Second Year—Popularity	Calling Fishers Sermon on the Mount Widow's Son Lakeside Parables Jairus' Daughter
	Third Year—Opposition	Feeding Five Thousand Syrophoenician's Daughter Peter's Confession Transfiguration Good Samaritan
	Last Three Months—Persecution	Lazarus Ten Lepers Little Children Rich Young Ruler Zacchaeus
	Last Week—Passion Week	Mary's Anointing Triumphal Entry Ten Virgins Upper Room Crucifixion
R I S E N	**Forty Days—Alive Again**	Appearance to Two Appearance to Ten Appearance to Seven Appearance to Five Hundred Appearance to Eleven

PERIODS AND EVENTS OF THE LIFE OF CHRIST

Review this chart frequently and practice till you can repeat the seven periods and the thirty-five events without hesitation. If you do not remember all the events permanently, make it a point at least to remember the seven periods. Perhaps you will mark your study Bible as suggested on the next page. Then whenever you study any part of the Gospels, you will know instantly what period of Christ's life you are studying. This will help you to have a better understanding of the Master's ministry as a whole, and often it will also give you a better understanding of the particular passage that you are studying.

		MATTHEW	MARK	LUKE	JOHN
Y O U T H	Thirty Years • Preparation	1:1—4:11	1:1-13	1:1—4:13	1:1-51
M I N I S T R Y	First Year • Obscurity				2:1—4:54
	Second Year • Popularity	4:12—9:35	1:14—5:43	4:14—8:56	5:1-47
	Third Year • Opposition	9:36—18:35	6:1—9:50	9:1—13:21	6:1—10:39
	Last 3 Months • Persecution	19:1—20:34	10:1-52	13:22—19:27	10:40—11:57
	Last Week • Passion	21:1—27:66	11:1—15:47	19:28—23:56	12:1—19:42
R I S E N	Forty Days • Alive Again	28:1-20	16:1-20	24:1-53	20:1—21:25

THE LIFE OF CHRIST IN THE SCRIPTURES

This chart shows approximately what portions of the Gospels are devoted to each of the seven periods in Christ's life. Perhaps you will not care to memorize this, but will keep it at hand for ready reference.

Better still, you may mark in your study Bible each point at which one period ends and another begins. When a whole page falls within a single period, you may note that period at the top of the page: Preparation, First Year, or whatever it is. Then when you study any portion of the Gospels, a single glance will tell you what period of the Master's life you are considering. It is helpful to know that an event belongs to the year of Jesus' greatest popularity, for example, or to the year of growing opposition.

Remember that the Gospels do not always record events exactly in the order of their occurrence. Therefore it is not possible always to be sure exactly when one year of Jesus' ministry ends and another begins. The divisions indicated here may not be exactly correct, but they are close enough to be helpful in our study of the Life of Christ.

The Apostles and the Great Commission

Lesson 21

After rising from the dead, Jesus commissioned His apostles to give the whole world the good news of His victory and His offer of salvation.

THE APOSTLES

A. Who were the apostles?

1. First, they were twelve disciples whom Jesus chose early in His ministry (Luke 6:12, 13):

> **Simon and Andrew**
> **James and John**
> **Philip and Bartholomew**
> **Thomas and Matthew**
> **James and Thaddaeus**
> **Simon and Judas**

2. Note that two of them were named Simon: Simon Peter and Simon the Canaanite or Zealot. And two were named James. One was the fisherman James, who was the son of Zebedee and brother John; the other was James the son of Alphaeus. Mark calls him "the less," probably because he was younger or shorter than the other James. There were also two apostles named Judas. See the next paragraph.

3. Note also that one man may have two names, or even three. One of the Simons was also called Peter and Cephas, two names meaning a stone (John 1:40-42). Thaddaeus was also called Lebbaeus, and Luke and John call him Judas (Luke 6:16; John 14:22). Many students think Bartholomew was the man John calls Nathanael (John 1:45-49; 21:2).

4. Judas hanged himself after betraying Christ. After Jesus ascended to heaven, the disciples, seeking divine help in their choice, named Matthias to take Judas' place (Acts 1:15-26).

5. Later Jesus chose Paul to be an apostle to the Gentiles (Acts 26:15-18).

B. What were the apostles?

1. The name *apostle* means one who is sent. Jesus gave it to twelve of His disciples because He sent them to be the leaders in carrying His message to the world.

2. The apostles were eyewitnesses. They saw Jesus after He rose from the dead. From their own personal knowledge they could testify to His resurrection.

3. The apostles were inspired: in a special way the Holy Spirit guided them into all truth and helped them remember what Jesus had taught them (John 14:26; 16:13). Infallibly, therefore, the apostles' teaching was Jesus' teaching.

4. The apostles had miraculous powers as evidence of the presence and power of the Holy Spirit.

THE GREAT COMMISSION

A. Jesus gave the great commission several times and in different ways. Memorize at least one of these:

Matthew 28:19, 20

Mark 16:15, 16
Acts 1:8

B. While this commission was given specifically to the apostles, the other early Christians helped to carry it out, and every Christian today is expected to do his part. But since Christians today are not inspired as the apostles were, every Christian must be careful to teach just what the inspired apostles taught.

QUESTIONS

1. What is the meaning of the word "apostle"?

_____

2. Why were Jesus's apostles so called?

_____

_____

3. In what ways were the apostles of Jesus specially qualified for the work the Master gave them to do?

_____

_____

_____

4. Quote the great commission Jesus gave to His apostles. Choose any one of the several ways in which He gave it.

_____

_____

_____

_____

_____

_____

_____

5. Do you think all Christians ought to have a part in carrying out this order?

_____

6. Name the twelve original apostles, giving two or three names to one apostle when you can.

_____

_____

_____

_____

_____

_____

_____

_____

_____

_____

7. Name two other apostles.

_____

8. How could other people tell that the Holy Spirit was with the apostles in a special way?

_____

_____

_____

REVIEW

Since this is a short lesson, you will have time for review. Look over the preceding lessons and spend some time with those of which your recollection is not very clear.

81

THERE WERE TWELVE DISCIPLES

Anon.

GEORGE A. MINOR

There were twelve dis-ci-ples Je-sus called to help Him: Si-mon Pe-ter,

An-drew, James, his bro-ther John; Phil-ip, Thom-as, Mat-thew,

James, the son of Al-pheus, Thad-deus, Si-mon, Ju-das, And Bar-thol-o-mew.

CHORUS

He has called us too, He has called us too; We are His dis-ci-

ples, I am one and you. ples, We His work must do.

Beginnings of the Church

Lesson 22

THE BEGINNING IN JERUSALEM

A. The First Day

The church began its work on the Day of Pentecost, fifty days after Jesus rose from the dead and ten days after He ascended to heaven. Following His instructions, the apostles were waiting in Jerusalem. Jews from many nations gathered there to celebrate the feast of Pentecost, one of their three great festivals. By our modern method of counting time, it probably was early in June, A.D. 30.

1. *The coming of the Holy Spirit.* With a sound like that of a great wind and with an appearance like tongues of fire, the Holy Spirit came to the apostles. He guided their thoughts as Jesus had promised (John 16:13, 14). He also enabled the apostles to speak in foreign languages so that Jews from many countries could hear the message in their own tongues (Acts 2:1-11).

2. *The message and the result.* Part of what Peter said is recorded. He cited Old Testament prophecies to show that the Christ could not be held by death. Then he gave the testimony of the apostles that Jesus had risen. On this basis he declared that Jesus was the Christ. Many of the hearers had consented to the crucifixion of Jesus a few weeks before. Conscience-stricken, they asked what they should do. Peter replied, "Repent, and be baptized every one of you in the name of Jesus Christ for the remission of sins, and ye shall receive the gift of the Holy Ghost." Three thousand people responded and were baptized.

B. Continuing Growth

As the apostles continued to preach the same message, other thousands responded. The number of men reached five thousand (Acts 4:4), and then even more multitudes were added (Acts 5:14). Even many of the priests became followers of Jesus (Acts 6:7), though the priests had taken the lead in demanding His death.

C. Some Incidents in Jerusalem

1. *Sharing of possessions.* Christians considered that their possessions belonged to their brethren as much as to them. Many sold property in order to care for the needy (Acts 2:44, 45; 4:32-37).

It should be noted that this was not communism in the modern sense. Private property continued to be held, but gifts were made voluntarily.

2. *Hypocrites.* As in other times, there were some who were less interested in giving than in getting credit for giving. Such were Ananias and Sapphira (Acts 5:1-10).

3. *Persecution.* As Jesus had foretold, those who had crucified Him soon began to persecute the apostles who declared He had risen. Acts 4 records an example. Imprisonment and beating were frequent, and it is thought that all of the apostles except John finally died for their faith.

4. *The seven.* There were many needy among the thousands of believers in

83

Jerusalem. Seven men were chosen to distribute to them the gifts made for that purpose (Acts 6:1-6). These seven are often called the first deacons, though the Bible does not give them that name, Among them were Stephen and Philip, who became noted evangelists. (This was not the apostle Philip, but another man of the same name.)

5. *Stephen.* Especially bitter was the opposition aroused by Stephen's vigorous teaching. Finding his arguments too much for them, his opponents finally resorted to violence and stoned him to death. He was the first follower of Jesus to die for the faith (Acts 6:8—7:60).

BEGINNINGS IN JUDEA AND SAMARIA

A. Scattered Disciples

With the stoning of Stephen, persecution became so violent that the disciples scattered from Jerusalem to save their lives. But wherever they went they took the story of Jesus and won others to Him (Acts 8:1-4).

B. Philip

Philip did a splendid evangelistic work in Samaria (Acts 8:4-13). Then an angel sent him to meet and convert an Ethiopian on the way to Gaza (Acts 8:26-39). Afterward he preached in Azotus and other cities as he went to Caesarea (Acts 8:40). See map on page 65.

C. Peter

With John, Peter toured Samaria with the gospel (Acts 8:14-25). Afterward he preached at various points in Judea. At Lydda he brought healing to Aeneas; at Joppa he raised Tabitha from the dead (Acts 9:32-43).

BEGINNINGS AMONG THE GENTILES

At first the gospel was preached only to Jews and to Samaritans, who were partly Jewish by race and by faith. But Jesus intended His message for the whole world.

A. Cornelius

By special revelations, God sent Peter to Caesarea to give the gospel to Cornelius, a devout Roman officer (Acts 10). Cornelius probably was the first Gentile follower of Christ.

B. Antioch

In the city of Antioch, three hundred miles north of Jerusalem, disciples preached freely to Gentiles. A great church grew up there, including both Jews and Gentiles. There the disciples were first called Christians (Acts 11:19-26).

C. Conversion of Saul

Very important to the growth of the church among Gentiles was the conversion of Saul, later known as Paul (Acts 9:1-20). Though he was a Jew, Jesus chose him to be a special apostle to Gentiles.

QUESTIONS

1. When did the church begin its work?

_____

_____

2. Who was the first Christian to be put to death for his faith?

_____

3. When persecution drove the Christians out of Jerusalem, what did they do?

_____

4. On the map on the opposite page, find the following places and write in the name of each one:

   a. The city where the church began its work.
   b. The area around that city, to which the gospel soon spread.
   c. The area where Philip was working when God's angel sent him to meet an Ethiopian.
   d. The town toward which the Ethiopian was traveling when he met Philip.
   e. The town where Tabitha was raised from the dead.
   f. The town where Cornelius heard the gospel.
   g. The city where the disciples were first called Christians.

84

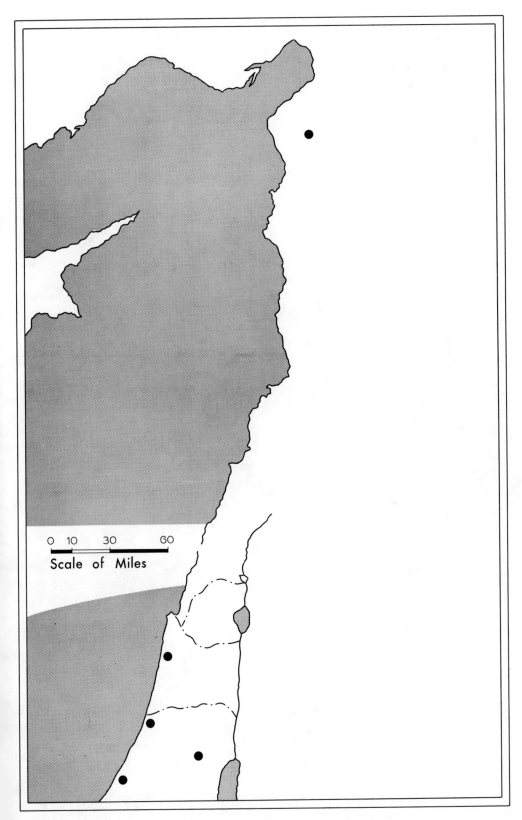

O   10   30   GO
Scale   of   Miles

New Life in Christ | Lesson 23

A NEW CREATURE

"If any man be in Christ, he is a new creature" (2 Corinthians 5:17). When a worldly man becomes a Christian, all phases of his life are new.

A. A New Standard

Remembering that in all the centuries no one has found a flaw in the perfect Christ, we make Him our standard. We try to be, and lead others to be, not only Christian but Christlike. In every decision we ask, "What would Jesus do?"

B. A New Hope

Most men have hope, but some have hope based on nothing but their own wish. Our hope is based on God's Word. He has promised forgiveness of sins, strength to overcome temptation, and eternal life to the faithful. We cannot create or earn any of these for ourselves, but we can trust in God to supply them.

C. A New Outlook

Even if we have all the world can give, the worldly outlook is short. It cannot reach beyond the grave. In Christ our outlook expands to include all eternity.

D. A New Incentive

Disappointments and disillusionment come to all. When everything seems to go wrong, the worldly man may say, "What's the use?" But to the Christian a disappointment is only a delay of blessings hoped for. Even when the world has done its worst we have an incentive to go on, for our greatest hope lies beyond this world.

E. A New Purpose

Worldly people have selfish purposes, but Christians know it is more blessed to give than to receive. Our purpose is to serve and please Him who loved us enough to die for us.

F. A New Reward

The world may offer riches, fame, power, learning, social achievement, and other desirable things; but it cannot offer what God offers to those in Christ—a forgiven life, a transformed life, eternal life, victory over sin and death, a home in heaven.

G. New Duties

We are saved to serve—not to serve ourselves, but to serve others. We imitate Him who "came not to be ministered unto, but to minister" (Mark 10:45). Attendance at the house of God, helping the needy in the name of Christ, and giving the gospel to others are some of the duties of a Christian.

H. New Obligations

In Christ we have become children of God. We owe our Father reverence, loyalty, service, and love. But these obligations are a joy rather than a burden, an opportunity rather than a hardship.

I. New Behavior

Wrongdoing of any kind is incompatible with our new life in Christ. We try to do always what is pleasing to the Master who has given us life. Purity, honesty, justice, unselfishness, charity, love, and service take on new importance.

NEW LIFE AND THE CHRISTIAN ORDINANCES

The Christian ordinances of baptism and the Lord's Supper are vitally related to new life in Christ. Baptism stands at the beginning of new life; the Lord's Supper provides continuing nourishment.

A. Baptism

1. *Authority for baptism.* In speaking of ordinances of the church, we mean that they were ordained *for* the church, not that they were ordained *by* the church. Both baptism and the Lord's Supper were ordained by Christ himself. We find authority for baptism in Matthew 28:18-20; Mark 16:15, 16; Acts 2:38. Study these carefully.

2. *Meaning of baptism.* Baptism means that a past life of sin is buried and a new life of doing right is beginning, with all the new things mentioned in the first part of this lesson. Study this idea carefully in Romans 6:1-14.

B. The Lord's Supper

1. *Authority for the Lord's Supper.* Like baptism, the Lord's Supper was ordained by Jesus himself. He said, "This do in remembrance of me." Study the origin of this ordinance in Matthew 26:26-28; Mark 14:22-25; Luke 22:15-20; 1 Corinthians 11:23-26.

2. *Meaning of the Lord's Supper.*

a. The Lord's Supper means that Jesus sacrificed His own body and shed His own blood for us (Matthew 26:26-28; 1 Corinthians 11:23-25).

b. It means that we remember His sacrifice with humility and gratitude, and proclaim it to others who need His salvation (1 Corinthians 11:26). If we are sincere in this, it certainly means that we renew our determination to give ourselves wholly to Him.

c. It means that we nourish and strengthen the new life we have in Him.

Study this idea in John 6:47-58. In taking of Christ's body and blood, if we are sincere and earnest, we take of His nature and become more Christlike.

QUESTIONS

1. List as many as you can of the new things belonging to a "new creature" in Christ.

_____

_____

_____

_____

_____

_____

_____

_____

_____

_____

2. Explain what Christian baptism has to do with the new life in Christ.

_____

_____

_____

_____

_____

3. Explain what the Lord's Supper has to do with the new life in Christ.

_____

_____

_____

_____

_____

88

Life of Paul
Part One

Lesson 24

In the recorded history of the early church, no one is more prominent than the apostle Paul. In the book of Acts, sixteen of the twenty-eight chapters are devoted mainly to his work. Of twenty-one letters in the New Testament, thirteen or fourteen are his. We cannot say he did more than all the other apostles, but we know more about what he did.

We do not know why this great man had two names, Saul and Paul. But it is evident that he is called Saul in the early parts of Acts and Paul in the latter part. The change comes in Act 13:9.

For our study, the life of Paul is divided into six periods:

1. **Saul the student**
2. **Saul the persecutor**
3. **Saul the convert**
4. **Paul the missionary**
5. **Paul the author**
6. **Paul the martyr**

Three of these periods will be considered in this lesson.

SAUL THE STUDENT

A. The Student in Tarsus

Saul was born in Tarsus, a city of Asia Minor. It was a Jewish custom to teach every boy a trade, and Saul became a tentmaker. Later he often supported himself by that trade while carrying on his evangelistic work. No doubt he was taught the Old Testament Scriptures both at home and in the synagogue. Even at this early age and in a heathen city, he may have been taught the strict ways of the Pharisees (Acts 23:6).

B. The Student in Jerusalem

For advanced study Saul went to Jerusalem, perhaps in his early teens. There he studied under Gamaliel (Acts 22:3), one of the most noted teachers and a member of the supreme council of the Jews. It was Gamaliel who later moved the council to save the lives of the apostles (Acts 5:33-40).

SAUL THE PERSECUTOR

Gamaliel's tolerant view of the apostles' work was not reflected in his student Saul. Being exceedingly zealous for the Jewish faith. Saul became one of the most fanatical of persecutors.

A. The Stoning of Stephen

For some reason Saul did not himself throw stones at Stephen, but he gave hearty consent and held the robes of his companions while they stoned Stephen to death (Acts 7:58—8:1).

B. Persecution in Jerusalem

After the death of Stephen, Saul took a furious part in arresting disciples in Jerusalem (Acts 8:3). He later said this persecution was "beyond measure" (Galatians 1:13) and a very great sin (1 Timothy 1:12-15).

C. The Trip to Damascus

Not content to persecute disciples in Jerusalem, Saul asked the priests to authorize him to arrest Jewish disciples in foreign cities. He was sent to Damascus to seek out followers of Jesus and bring them back in chains (Acts 9:1, 2).

SAUL THE CONVERT

A. On the Way to Damascus

Before he reached Damascus, Saul had a miraculous experience. The Christ appeared to him, convincing him that he was opposing the very Messiah whom he and all the Jews expected (Acts 9:1-8). Later Paul explained that Jesus appeared thus to make him a witness and an apostle (Acts 26:12-18).

B. In Damascus

Blinded by the brilliant vision of Jesus, Saul remained blind in Damascus for three days. Then the Lord sent a disciple named Ananias to restore his sight. Ananias then said, "Arise, and be baptized, and wash away thy sins, calling on the name of the Lord" (Acts 9:8-18; 22:11-16).

C. Saul as a New Christian

Saul spent two or three years in Arabia and Damascus. He left the city for a time, perhaps to find a quiet place where he could pray for guidance and restudy the Old Testament in the light of the truth he had learned about Christ. But whenever he had the opportunity, he now proclaimed the gospel he had opposed—proclaimed it so forcefully that the Jews determined to kill him. They enlisted the help of the governor of Damascus, but Saul escaped and returned to Jerusalem. There he was hated by his former companions and feared by the disciples he once had sought to arrest and injure. The former prosecutor now was bitterly persecuted.

D. Saul the Fugitive

Thanks to kindly Barnabas, the disciples at Jerusalem finally accepted Saul. But the Jews plotted to kill him, so he fled back home to Tarsus. From there Barnabas summoned him to help in the rapidly growing church in Antioch. It was Antioch that became the base for Paul's famous missionary journeys.

QUESTIONS

1. List six periods of Paul's life.

_____

_____

_____

_____

_____

_____

2. Tell a little about each of the first three periods.

_____

_____

_____

_____

_____

_____

_____

_____

_____

_____

_____

3. On the next page, write in the names of all places named in this lesson. Draw a line tracing the movements of Paul from the time he left Tarsus as a student until he came to Antioch as a Christian worker.

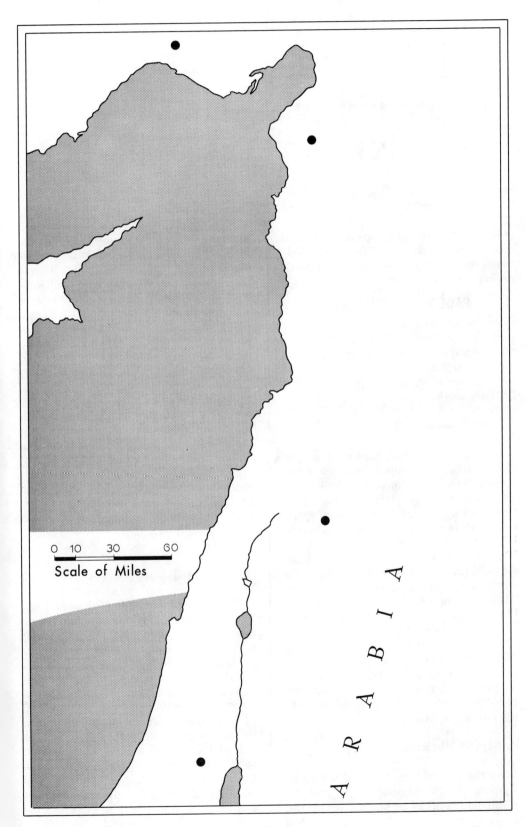

Life of Paul
Part Two

Lesson 25

Review the three periods of Paul's life covered in Lesson 24. This lesson continues with the fourth, fifth, and sixth periods.

PAUL THE MISSIONARY

For a year or more Saul taught in Antioch, and from that city he began his three famous missionary journeys. After these, the book of Acts records his eventful trip to Rome. Little is known of his later work.

A. First Missionary Journey
A.D. 45-49

Paul began his missionary work on the great island of Cyprus, not far from Antioch. There he converted the Roman governor, Sergius Paulus. From that time Saul was called Paul. From Cyprus he sailed north to the mainland. Moving inland through the mountains, he came to a city called by the same name as his starting point, Antioch. From there he went on to Iconium, Lystra, and Derbe. Then he turned back and visited each of these places again, giving additional teaching to the new Christians before he returned to his starting point. Read the record in Acts 13 and 14. Barnabas was Paul's companion on this journey, and on the first part of it they were accompanied by John Mark, who later wrote the Gospel of Mark.

B. Second Missionary Journey
A.D. 50-53

On the second tour Paul did not go to Cyrpus, but traveled by land to visit the mainland churches he had started on the first trip. Then he went on west to Troas, from which he sailed across the narrow sea to Macedonia. At Philippi Lydia was converted, then a jailer who had kept Paul in prison. Paul next preached in Thessalonica, then went on to Berea. Unbelieving Jews of Thessalonica opposed him bitterly in both places, and he went on to Athens, where he delivered his famous sermon on Mars' Hill. After that he worked a year and a half in Corinth, building a large church in a city noted for its wickedness. From Corinth he turned eastward, stopping briefly at Ephesus and probably attending a Jewish feast at Jerusalem before returning to Antioch. Paul and Silas began this journey together. Timothy joined them at Lystra, and Luke was added to the party in Troas. This journey is recorded in Acts 15:36—18:22.

C. Third Missionary Journey
A.D. 54-58

On the third journey, Paul went from Antioch through the "upper coasts" or mountains of Asia Minor (Acts 19:1), perhaps revisiting churches started on his first trip. Then he settled at Ephesus for about three years. Afterward he visited the churches in Macedonia and Greece, then sailed from Philippi by way of Troas and Miletus to Caesarea. From there he went on to Jerusalem to attend one of the Jewish feasts. There a mob tried to kill him, but he was rescued by Roman soldiers stationed near the temple. The Roman governor returned him to Caesarea, but kept him in prison for two years, A.D. 58-60. On the latter part of this trip Luke was with Paul. Read the account in chapters 19—24 of Acts.

D. The Trip to Rome—A.D. 60-61

Seeing no hope of justice in Caesarea, Paul appealed to the Roman emperor. The governor then sent him to Rome for judgment. After a stormy voyage, the ship was wrecked on the island of Melita, or Malta as it is now called. The passengers spent the rest of the winter there and then took another ship to Puteoli, from which they proceeded to Rome on foot. Paul was a prisoner in Rome for two years, A.D. 61-63, and at that point the book of Acts ends. Luke was with Paul on this eventful trip. See the record in the last two chapters of Acts.

E. Later Travels—A.D. 63-68

The book of Acts ends with Paul a prisoner in Rome, but in the letters to Timothy and Titus there are hints that lead many scholars to think he was released and resumed his travels, revisiting churches in Asia and Macedonia as well as teaching on the island of Crete. Old tradition indicates that he also went to Spain.

PAUL THE AUTHOR

Paul wrote about half the books of the New Testament—thirteen or fourteen. Some were written during busy missionary tours, others while he was a prisoner in Rome. This therefore is not really another period, but another activity of his missionary period.

Some of his letters such as Romans and Thessalonians, were written to churches. Others were written to individuals, such as Timothy, Titus, and Philemon.

PAUL THE MARTYR
A.D. 68

In A.D. 64 the Roman emperor, Nero, launched a great persecution against the Christians, whom he accused of starting a disastrous fire in Rome. The persecution continued about four years. Tradition has it that Paul was arrested and put to death near the end of this time.

LATER WORK OF JOHN

John probably is the only one of the apostles who lived and worked for a long time after Paul died. Early Christian writings outside the Bible indicate that he lived in Ephesus after Jerusalem was destroyed in A.D. 70. Between 70 and 100 John wrote his Gospel, three letters, and Revelation. Some think all of these were written between 90 and 100.

QUESTIONS

1. On one map on the next page, draw lines to trace Paul's first and second missionary journeys.

2. Use the other map to trace his third journey and trip to Rome.

3. Name the New Testament books Paul wrote. See Lesson 5 if necessary.

_____

_____

_____

_____

_____

_____

_____

_____

_____

_____

_____

_____

_____

4. According to tradition, how did Paul's life end?

_____

5. Locate Ephesus, where John probably lived, and the island of Patmos, where he was a prisoner when he wrote the book of Revelation.

94

The Bible for the Whole World

Lesson 26

THE DIVINE PURPOSE

A. God's purpose is to bless the whole world.

1. He chose Abraham for this purpose (Genesis 22:17, 18).

2. Because He loved the whole world, He sent His Son to redeem it (John 3:16).

3. The best of all nations shall share His eternal home (Revelation 21:23-27).

B. Christ sent His people to teach the whole world.

1. The gospel is for every creature (Mark 16:15, 16).

2. Every teaching of Christ is for all nations (Matthew 28:19, 20).

MISSIONARY EXAMPLES

A. Christ himself was a missionary.

1. The word *missionary* comes from a Latin word that means *send*. Christ was sent to reveal God's will as well as to redeem, and He sends His people in like manner (John 20:21).

2. His people should imitate Him in their devotion to God's will and to making it known.

B. The chief writer of the New Testament was a missionary.

1. Paul wrote about half the books of the New Testament.

2. This is some indication of the extent of his missionary work, for he wrote mostly to people and churches involved in that work.

C. Christians generally were missionaries in New Testament times.

1. Scattered from Jerusalem, they went everywhere preaching the word (Acts 8:4).

2. Examples of Christian teachers are Ananias of Damascus (Acts 22:10-16) and Aquila and Priscilla (Acts 18:24-26).

D. The New Testament is a missionary book.

1. The Gospels tell the story of Christ's own mission in the world.

2. Acts tells of the missionary work of the church.

3. Many letters were written by missionaries to their mission fields.

4. Revelation 22:17 urges those who respond to God's call to extend that call to others.

THE NEED OF THE WORLD

A. The world desperately needs the Word of God.

1. Though nature is a partial revelation of God, people without His Word drift farther and farther from Him (Romans 1:18-25).

2. All have sinned, and the wages of sin is death (Romans 3:23; 6:23).

B. The gospel is the power of God unto salvation (Romans 1:16).

1. If God's people had not brought it to us or to our ancestors in bygone years, we could have no hope of salvation.

2. If we do not continue to take it to others, countless millions will be lost.

THE WORD
AND THE WORLD TODAY

A. What has been accomplished

1. There is hardly a country in the world where the gospel has not been heard by some.

2. Thousands of missionaries are constantly at work to reach others.

3. Parts of the Bible have been translated into more than a thousand languages.

B. What remains to be done

1. Probably two-thirds of the world's people are not Christian.

2. Many areas, such as some African countries, have been touched but slightly by Christian teaching.

3. A new start may sometime be possible in populous countries where communist governments have bitterly opposed Christianity.

4. In all lands, most Christians have neighbors who are not Christians. There is work to be done next door as well as around the world.

QUESTIONS

1. Give some examples of missionary work recorded in the New Testament.

_____

_____

_____

_____

_____

_____

_____

2. In what ways is the New Testament a missionary book?

_____

_____

_____

_____

_____

_____

_____

3. Why does the world need God's Word?

_____

_____

_____

4. What has been accomplished in the effort to give the Bible to the whole world?

_____

_____

_____

_____

_____

5. What remains to be done?

_____

_____

_____

_____